WORLD WITHIN A SONG

ALSO BY JEFF TWEEDY

How to Write One Song
Let's Go (So We Can Get Back)

WORLD WITHIN A SONG

Music That Changed My Life
and Life That Changed My Music

JEFF TWEEDY

DUTTON

DUTTON

An imprint of Penguin Random House LLC
penguinrandomhouse.com

DUTTON and the D colophon are registered trademarks
of Penguin Random House LLC.

Interior art © snorks/Shutterstock.com

LIBRARY OF CONGRESS CATALOGING-IN-PUBLICATION DATA
Names: Tweedy, Jeff, 1967– author.
Title: World within a song: music that changed my life and
life that changed my music / Jeff Tweedy.
Description: [1.] | New York: Dutton, 2023.
Identifiers: LCCN 2023028471 (print) | LCCN 2023028472 (ebook) |
ISBN 9780593472521 (hardcover) | ISBN 9780593472538 (ebook)
Subjects: LCSH: Tweedy, Jeff, 1967– | Popular music—Anecdotes. |
Alternative rock musicians—United States—Biography. |
Alternative country musicians—United States—Biography. |
LCGFT: Autobiographies.
Classification: LCC ML420.T954 A3 2023 (print) |
LCC ML420.T954 (ebook) | DDC 782.42166092 [B]—dc23/eng/20230804
LC record available at https://lccn.loc.gov/2023028471
LC ebook record available at https://lccn.loc.gov/2023028472
9780593475645 (signed edition)
9780593475652 (B&N signed edition)

Printed in the United States of America

1st Printing

BOOK DESIGN BY ASHLEY TUCKER

To Susie, Spencer, and Sammy

CONTENTS

LOOK . . .

I'M GOING TO LEVEL WITH YOU RIGHT OFF THE BAT. I don't know what I'm doing, and I probably don't have any business writing another book, much less one as conceptually conceived and philosophical as this one aims to be.

But the truth is, I should've written this book first, and I would have if I'd had any wherewithal and confidence from the get-go. So I wrote a memoir sort of by accident. Initially it was something proposed to me. Preposterous at first, considering I wasn't even half finished living my life by my own hopeful estimation. I was eventually convinced to give it a go, and I'm glad now that I was able to accept the task as a challenge as well as an opportunity to offer up a little advice in the form of "Here's some shit you might want to look out for if you're, like me, a human person trying not to suffer overly so" and "Hey, I'm a dumbass. Don't be a dumbass like me," along with a few "Well whaddaya know? I figured out some of this shit on my own, so you could try what worked for me so you don't have to go into the hospital and whatnot."

In the end I enjoyed it. I enjoyed it enough to write another book. This time I got a little closer to the stuff I think about the most and I allowed myself to revisit the topic I had the easiest time writing about in my memoir: the creative process. More specifically, I wrote about my own habit of intentionally making time for myself to spend a part of each day engaged with my imagination. I wrote about making stuff and how I think it's good and good for you.

I tried not to get too didactic or preachy in that book, but it was hard not to veer off into self-help-adjacent philosophy periodically. But honestly, I think it was the right thing to do. The way I see it, I'm lucky to be in a position to advocate for creativity as a live-well strategy. The world needs more of that type of thing, and I was happy to do it.

So that brings us to this book. The one you're holding or listening to right now. This book is the one I probably would have written first if I were more ambitious, and if I had been a little more clear-eyed about what I care most for in this world, and what I've thought about the most by far: other people's songs. And how much they have taught me about how to be human—how to think about myself and others. And how deeply personal and universally vast the experience of listening to almost anything with intent and openness can be. And most importantly, how songs absorb and enhance our own experiences and store our memories.

How did I come up with this particular list of songs? I could have easily chosen a thousand other songs to write about. And having finished that book, I would regret the omission of a thousand other songs. These are just the ones that came to me first. Besides, the specifics of the songs themselves aren't really the point. What's important to me to convey is how miraculous songs are. It doesn't matter how many people hear "A Day in the Life," there is only one version that belongs to you. Mine has little to do with yours. Our appraisals might align but I doubt your relationship to the song includes a memory of waiting for the doors to open at an all-ages Jodie Foster's Army concert on Laclede's Landing in St. Louis, with a flooding Mississippi River raging down Wharf Street and heaving up onto the steps of the Gateway Arch. Mind melting down on mushrooms, watching a husband-and-wife street-performing duo sing "A Day in the Life" while their toddler does laps around you keeping shockingly good time on a tambourine.

It'd be cool if we could see the worlds within the songs inside each other's heads. But I also love how impenetrable it all is. I love that what's mine can't be yours and we still get to call it ours. Songs are the essence of this condition. And in my opinion, they're the best way I know of to make peace with our lack of a shared consciousness.

Creating connection through music is my life's work. Truly. Still, what makes my thoughts on other people's songs worth investing in? Well, I'll tell you, if I hadn't written those other books, I'm not sure I'd be able to answer that. But what I've realized through sharing my thoughts and feelings in my books is that there are people out there having very similar thoughts and feelings. The lesson hasn't been that my perspective is so unique it must be shared so as to enlighten. It's more that I've learned that I'm not alone. I'm not a freak to care about this as much as I do.

The main response I get to the things I've written is the miraculous comment "I feel like I could have written that." It's a joyous discovery to realize that something as ego-driven and interior as a book can return from its visit to all the people it managed to reach in the world with the hopeful and humbling message that you've been understood. You've given someone else the words to name their own experiences. Wonders never cease.

A NOTE ON REMEMORIES

AS YOU PROGRESS THROUGH THIS BOOK, YOU'RE GO-ing to encounter some dreamlike passages recounting specific events in my life. I call them Rememories, and I've been writing down some of my most-often-shared life stories in that style for a few years now.

Their inclusion here has a couple of purposes. On one hand, I hope that they'll work as palate cleansers between chapters as we reemerge from the thick weeds of my internal and endless musing on the weight of songs, as we climb out of the "book-sized writing" language and look around for a little space to think.

But I also included them to illustrate how my deep immersion in music has shaped how I really think and remember things in "song-sized" thoughts and shapes. And how important it is to allow the things we love the most—the things we've contemplated the most thoughtfully and with the most empathy and compassion—to guide our hand when we're stumped.

I have very few strongly held beliefs. Among them is the conviction that loving one thing deeply and with ardor is the best way to open yourself up to the world. It's a bit counterintuitive, but I've seen it with my own eyes and felt it with my own heart. My obsession with music from a very early age had the potential to isolate and alienate me from the world at large. But I believe that by indulging that passion and focus, I found the only way into knowing what people live for.

Loving one thing completely becomes a love for all things, somehow. I've seen it in other people, too. And I've been able to communicate with them solely using the language I've learned from music to talk about, for instance, other art, gardening, coaching college basketball, war correspondence . . . you get the idea.

So I've included these memories, sung to the tunes swirling around my own mind. They remind me of what I'm getting at and how beautifully intertwined it all becomes over time when you open up and allow the world to pour in both directions at once, inward and outward.

WORLD WITHIN A SONG

SMOKE ON THE WATER

I'D LOVE TO CLAIM THAT AT THE AGE OF SIX, HEAR-ing the brief passage of Mozart (incorrectly identified as Rachmaninoff) performed in the movie *Willy Wonka and the Chocolate Factory* was the catalyst that set me on my way to a lifetime of music-making . . . or that I was somehow introduced to some Jacques Brel or Leonard Cohen by an eccentric den mother at a Cub Scout meeting and I never looked back, having immediately absorbed the nuance and depth of the wordplay and how the simple melodic arcs embrace eternity . . .

In fact, I'd much prefer to have you believe just about anything other than what truthfully made the first dent in my musical mind. That's because the truth is that it was "Smoke on the Water" by Deep Purple. It kills me to admit this for a lot of reasons. Foremost of which is the fact that as I grew older and as this song maintained an ominous loitering presence on the airwaves of St.

Louis rock radio, it became more and more indefensible as something I could admit to myself that I liked.

Things were different then. Without much else to distinguish ourselves from each other as adolescents (fewer clothing options, same shoes, our moms all cut our hair), we were forced to broadcast our allegiances (jock, nerd, sosh, etc.) by the music we professed to love. By the time I was a full-blown teenager, this bong-bruised, coughed-up lung of a song had evolved, in terms of the people who liked it at the time, to signify a distinct type of danger to a sensitive boy like myself. Kind of the way some insects develop brightly colored wings to tell predators, "Trust me, you're better off not fucking with me." This song came to indicate a certain toxicity, in other words.

But alas, I cannot deny its importance to me, and countless others, as a budding musician. Because the fact is, this riff (I'm not even sure I could speak to the rest of the song considering how much I've avoided it in the nearly fifty years since my first introduction; I know it has something to do with Frank Zappa and some semiautobiographical band exploit, but to me, even if I HAD paid more attention to the words, this riff is so dunderheaded and massive it blots out the sun—hippie mumbo jumbo lyrics don't stand a chance) . . . this riff is absolutely the first thing I ever played on a guitar, back when I was seven or eight years old. This, my friends, was the "Seven Nation Army" of my day. The likelihood you could teach yourself these four notes on the bottom string of a guitar within a few minutes was very very high.

So I must bow to the rock gods. Who cares if it took a riff so demeaning and dumb to instill a little belief in myself as a potential musician? We all start somewhere. I started with "Smoke on the" goddamn "Water."

2

LONG TALL GLASSES

YOU KNOW, NOT EVERYTHING THAT ENDS UP HAVING
a profound influence in your life is easily identified as
enjoyable. In fact, I think I could safely argue that it's
pretty rare for life lessons to be imparted free of concern
and full of mirth. Songs, or at least most of the songs
I've chosen to talk about here, are unique in that way.
They really can teach with serenity, form wisdom while
the mind drifts carelessly, or even shine a little light
into the dark corners of a banging head.

But not always. There are still important kernels of
knowledge that can only be whipped into us through
discomforting experience. Take this Leo Sayer song, for
example. Sure, it seems pleasant enough. And taken as a
single dose, I'm almost certain one would recover fairly
quickly from its mild toxins. But let's take this same
song and play it . . . oh . . . let's say roughly forty-five
times between six P.M. and nine P.M. on weekday

evenings, and upward of seventy times a day on the weekends. Let's continue this ritual for several months and try to imagine the world-warping effect this little ditty might have on one's psyche.

If it weren't for the fact that I believe my father sincerely enjoyed such a routine, I would find it easy to subscribe to the possibility that the method behind such madness was in service to a DARPA program set up by the DOD to study the mind-altering potential inherent in repeated exposure to a single insipid storytelling pop song.

If you're unfamiliar with the song . . . first of all, CONGRATULATIONS . . . but I should give you a little outline of what its "deal" is. It's a musical tale of a man down on his luck (natch) who stumbles upon an establishment offering up food and drink to one and all. It goes on to describe said spread (which is where he unloads one of the most diabolically infuriating rhymes of all time: "There was ham and there was turkey / There was caviar / And long tall glasses / With wine up to . . . YAR"). It ambles along for a while before we get to the kicker: If he wants to partake in the bounty before him, he's gonna have to dance for it. But alas, he doesn't know how to dance, and he's sad, the music is sad, we're sad . . . but then . . . but THEN . . . Spoiler alert: Turns out he CAN dance after all.

Incredible. At this point in the song the refrain "You know I CAN'T dance," sung like a donkey doing a

Bogart impression, becomes "I CAN dance!" This is the moment where my beer maudlin-ed father would jump out of his chair and spill his Pabst (Extra Light) dancing and bellowing along. "I CAN DANCE!" EVERY. SINGLE. TIME.

So what did I learn from this hardship? Why am I writing about this particular song in a book designed to highlight the inspiration I've taken from the music I've consumed?

Well, I guess I'm not sure how to answer that. But I can tell you that at the time this was all happening, I was sure I was learning about things I would never do and ways that I would never be. As a musician, as a songwriter, as a father, and as a human, I guess.

Every now and then I throw this song on, and as I sit and listen, as this smug bauble of pop arcana winds its way through the paths in my mind that it's beaten down to dust, the memories of my father become so vivid I swear I can smell him. I am with him again. But this time without judgment. Only joy for his joy. Name something else in the world that can do that.

SPITTING ON THE
BAR MIRROR

REMEMBERING THAT OUR HOUSE, WHICH MY PARENTS claimed may have been a speakeasy at one time, had a bar in the basement, and a separate entrance, which checks out with its maybe being a place to drink during prohibition. It wasn't a totally finished basement, but it had an old, long bar, with a big mirror behind it, almost like an old saloon.

Bringing my friend downstairs and revealing my plan . . . I had seen a movie when I was a little kid where the bad guy spit at the bartender and spit on the mirror behind the bar. Based on this movie, my friend and I spent an entire afternoon running up to the bar, jumping on a bar stool, and spitting on the mirror behind the bar.

My father reacting in horror when he came home and saw the mirror, covered in our spit. I think that was the only time that he ever spanked me.

TAKIN' CARE OF BUSINESS

IF YOU WERE A KID IN THE SEVENTIES AND HAD OLDER cousins who played guitar, there's a solid chance that your first exposure to a lot of songs was through an impromptu performance at a family barbecue or some other type of family get-together. And if you were like me, a little sheltered and radio-less, the idea that your cousins were incredible songwriters and musicians might have taken a strong hold.

For much of my childhood, I marveled at this song and how insanely good it was, and how incredible it was that my cousin (BeBo, we called him) wrote this masterpiece. This was my favorite of HIS songs. I'm not accusing him of plagiarism. I mean, it wasn't like he had a moral obligation to back-announce his selections on any given evening so that his weird little cousin wouldn't get the wrong idea about who wrote his material.

Thinking now about how many great songs he used

to play, I was tempted to write about Jim Croce and "Bad, Bad Leroy Brown" too, but then I remembered the night that particular illusion was destroyed by a newscast reporting on Croce's untimely death in a plane crash. As a montage of images from his career played over a medley of his hits, I put two and two together and figured out that Jim Croce was probably the one who wrote "Leroy Brown." But since they didn't play any Bachman-Turner Overdrive, I was able to retain my pride in being related to the guy who wrote "Takin' Care of Business."

It was a sweet time. I'm not particularly nostalgic for that era of my childhood, but I do appreciate that this way of hearing a song for the first time probably doesn't happen as much anymore. Maybe it does . . . I really don't know . . . but it seems like something that might have been extinguished by the relatively new relationship everyone has with music these days. It's omnipresent in all of our lives. Everyone is walking around with access to so much music it's hard to believe that when I finally did get a radio (one conveniently "fell off a train" at my dad's work somewhere around my ninth birthday), I used to stay up for hours hoping to hear a song a DJ might or might not ever play again, mostly because I didn't catch the name of the artist the first time around.

I truly hope that people still play songs for their extended younger kin without letting on who wrote what. Because a song's magic really does deserve to be spread around, and part ownership should definitely belong to whoever can conjure it up in front of any size audience spontaneously (okay, setting aside the chaotic publishing ramifications, of course).

The fact is, this song is probably one of the most important songs in my life. Because cousin BeBo took the time to learn it and sing it to his friends and family, and because it looked like a thing someone could do—write a song and sing it—I was convinced forever that writing a song and singing it was not only a way to tap into the divine, it was normal.

I'm not sure I've ever truly processed this song as anyone's other than my cousin's. And as I got older, a lot of people I knew would make fun of this band and this song. But there must be something to be said for the fact that every band I've ever been in knows this song. And how it's a not uncommon occurrence for someone to launch into this song for no particular reason at all during a sound check or rehearsal, to smiles all around when everyone joins in. In fact, there's a running gag at the Wilco headquarters and recording studio, the Loft. Whenever I try out a new guitar, the opening riff of "TCB" comes first. Mark Greenberg, our studio manager, drops whatever he's doing and runs to the nearest piano to play the pulsing high-register eighth notes that complete the ROCK!

It's pure joy every time. Any song that can put that much joy in the world deserves my respect.

Thank you, BeBo.

DON'T THINK TWICE, IT'S ALL RIGHT

BOB DYLAN. BOB. DYLAN. IS THERE ANYONE ELSE YOU can refer to with either of their names and be as sure someone will understand who you're talking about? I can't think of anyone. It's usually one or the other. Groucho Marx? I'll give you Groucho, but Marx is definitely a different dude. Anyway, what's left to say about Bob Dylan? Well, judging by the amount of shit written about him every year, a lot! Between the two big British rock mags, *Uncut* and *Mojo*, one or the other will put him on the cover at least once every six months. Presumably because people still can't get enough of the guy. Which makes sense, because I can't get enough of the guy, either.

In fact, I can't think of any other artist I love more. And whether they admit it or not (or in some cases whether or not they're even aware of it), I believe every songwriter wants some piece of what Dylan has. His poetic gifts, his prolificacy, his longevity, his mystique, his hair! He's like the guy who invented walking upright. Even if you don't know who he is, you should know you owe him a lot. I mean, I sure do. To Dylan, that is. And also the guy who invented walking upright.

So when it comes to all of the many attributes of Dylan's one could list or wish to possess, I would put myself down as a songwriter who longs for them all. Let's ignore the others who insist they are immune to the Dylan influence or that they exist freestanding apart from the world he has made for all of us song people. Because I, for one, think they are deluded poopie heads.

I could have easily chosen only Dylan songs to write about if I were only concentrating on the criterion of importance to my personal development as a writer of songs . . . but "Don't Think Twice" is the first Dylan song I fell for, so it's the one I'm including.

It was originally released on the album *The Free-wheelin' Bob Dylan*, in 1963. About four years before I was born. I first heard it on *Bob Dylan's Greatest Hits Vol. II*, which came out in '71. So I'm guessing I got this record in a cache of handed-down vinyl a few years after that. That puts us at around 1974. And that puts me at around seven years old. I mention all of this not to buff my bona fide badge as a precocious and intellectually curious youngster but because I still think about it, and I can still feel how deeply I identified with this song so quickly and how strange that is.

I once loved a woman
A child I am told
I gave her my heart but she wanted my soul

How does a seven-year-old hear that and say, "THAT'S ME!"? But I did. I did and I still do. How? My best guess now as to why a song kissing off a lover like this one would resonate with just about anyone is the fact that, at its core, it's saying, "I'll be okay. I'm alienated and maybe a bit angry that I could be treated so poorly, but guess what, I'm the one with the road in front of me. I am free."

How alienated could I have been as a seven-year-old to so desperately need to hear a Nixonian "You're not going to have me to kick around anymore" lyric as something more liberating than self-pitying? The answer is obviously VERY! I was born alienated, I think. And when I heard this song, it was maybe the first time I heard that hurt sung to a melody I could understand.

IS THERE A MERIT BADGE
FOR SHAME?

EVERY TIME SOMEONE ASKS ME IF I WAS EVER A BOY Scout, I say no. And then I feel compelled to tell them I never made it on account of being shamed out of the Cub Scouts.

Here's the story.

I was pretty excited to build a Pinewood Derby car when they handed out the kits at our "den" meeting. It was supposed to be a father-son project, but (knowing how unlikely that scenario would be based on past experiences) I put it all together by myself when I got home.

Either my mom really got on my dad's case or my dad really did feel sorry for me when he saw my attempt at building a "race car." Or it's possible some combination of the above and his own competitive nature kicked in, because in a stunning reversal of attitude toward the whole idea, he committed to the undertaking with gusto.

Now, did that mean he took me down to an old workbench in the basement and carefully walked me through the steps of designing and shaping an aerodynamic miniature racing vehicle? No. If you were making a movie, I think this would be where you would cut together a montage of my father's coarse hands helping guide my chubby little fingers as they sand the contours of a Maserati out of a soft block of wood—paint being dabbed on my nose, heads tossed back laughing, sawdust falling to the floor, close-up on our eyes gliding along the sleek profile of a finished speedster.

But this is how it actually went. "BOY!! . . . BRING ME THAT DAMN 'CAR' YOU MADE DOWN HERE!! . . . NOW GO TO BED." Adding, "I get up before you know what day it is."

The next evening, Dad came home with a completely rebuilt masterpiece of engineering and design. Apparently, he had put a team of railroad technicians on the task. The axles were coated in graphite. They had hollowed out and filled an internal channel with mercury. And they had added a stack of tiny washers underneath the chassis so we could adjust the weight at the weigh-in, because they had determined being able to get as close as possible to the max weight would be the key to speed in a race being run with only gravity as fuel. To top it off, "my" car now sported a jaunty red, white, and blue paint job.

So far so good, right? Sure, some bonding with my

dad might have been nice, but this car really did "go like the dickens," as my dad would say. "Our" car destroyed the competition. Which, to be honest, mostly looked like my car had before my dad Manhattan Project–ed the shit out of that pathetic little chunk of crappy wood.

I admit it was really fun winning. And winning so handily made it extra fun. Mercilessly, one might say. It was a good night. And Dad was pretty excited to see the trophy "he" won when we got home. No, he did not attend. Need I remind you he got up "before the ass crack of dawn"?

Okay. The real trouble started a year later.

Same drill. The bonding part of the project was emphasized as the most important part. A new block of wood was issued with the clear directive that a new car must be built to legally enter the contest.

I gave my dad the materials, this time without even bothering to slap the wheels on the sucker, and I told him to put the A team on it. "What's wrong with the one from last year?" he asked. So I explained the rules to him. He stared back at me and sucked on his teeth for a few seconds, and then he said, "Well, gimme the old one to take along so we can remember what we did to make it so great."

Next evening he came home and handed me what was obviously the same car as last year, only now it was a glossy dark shade of blue. He winked. I nodded. He was an adult. I was just a kid. We're geniuses, we thought.

The only person I told about our masterful plot to sidestep the rules and dominate the field for a second year running was my best friend at the time—let's just call him "Kent."

Well, as luck would have it, Kent came in second place. And as I stood holding my trophy, I watched Kent with tears in his eyes walk around the track, past the rows of lunch tables, and directly up to the lectern where our scout leader was making some final announcements for the evening over the PA. I can still vividly see him pointing in my direction as a small group of adults began to gather around him. Kent was a rat, turns out.

I mean, he was right. And I was wrong. I understood that even then. But it's what the adults did next that I still have trouble believing. The scout leader leaned into the microphone and made a terse request for me to step up to the lectern. Which is where my trophy was taken from my hands and I was officially disqualified. In front of everyone in attendance. All of my classmates.

I was inconsolable. My mother was irate. At them, thank god.

My dad was asleep when we got home. Understandable, considering he'd had "a whole got-damned day by the time you lift your pretty head off of your pillow."

He never said much about it other than, "Some people take stupid shit way too seriously."

I was never sure if he was talking about them or himself.

MULL OF KINTYRE

NOT A LOT OF PEOPLE ARE FAMILIAR WITH THIS SONG outside of the UK. Or at least that was the case in the late seventies. No way of telling these days. For all I know, some chunk of this tune is being used on TikTok, triggering a massive uptick in bagpipe sales to bored tweens. I doubt it. But weirder things have happened. It is gorgeous. Stirring, even. And I might have thought to include it here because it does exactly that—it stirs something Scottish in me. Something deep and ancestral. But if I'm being honest, a lot of Paul McCartney's music would have come to mind before this one if I were picking songs to write about based solely on my appreciation for them as a songwriter. But there's a story inside this song I'd like to share.

In spite of having been a massive hit on the UK charts as a single, it had never been on an album until late 1978, when it got its album debut on *Wings Greatest*.

Which I'm guessing was some type of contractually obligated release, cobbled together for maximum Christmas sales. In other words, it never made its way onto a real album. But my story isn't that I found this cash grab of an album under the tree on Christmas morning and went on to fall in love with this oddly obscure track, which was a love letter to Sir Paul's home in the Scottish countryside. In fact, I had no knowledge this song or the *Wings Greatest* LP even existed until early summer 1979, when I received it as a gift from an unlikely source.

First, a little backstory.

There was a pivotal moment in my life I've written about before, which I'd like to recount here a bit as well—the catastrophic bicycle accident I had on the last day of school before summer break in 1979. In my memoir and elsewhere, I've often credited this terrible childhood event and the forced isolation that resulted from it (due to injuries sustained) as the main reason I learned how to play guitar. A skill that forever changed the trajectory of my life. This is a tangential story to that main narrative—a soft, sweet memory, but indelible nonetheless.

The friend I was with when this accident happened was a very different kind of kid than I was. He was more of a country kid. We didn't have a lot in common other than baseball, maybe. He was kind of an acquaintance, really, but we liked each other enough to "go bike riding" after school that day. So it wouldn't have been surprising to me at all if I had never seen him again after the trauma he went through, seeing me carted off to the hospital in the back of his neighbor's pickup truck with a blood-soaked towel wrapped around the gaping holes in my thigh. We'd been racing our bikes up and down a hill in front of his house. I had his little brother riding double behind me on a banana seat, clutching my ribs, when I crashed into a drainage ditch. His little brother walked away without a hair out of place. I got skewered by some rusty metal retaining rods sticking out of an old culvert. My friend rode up laughing at the spectacle of us sailing off of the end of his blacktopped cul-de-sac into oblivion. And then quickly went white when he saw my horrific wounds. That was the last time I saw him.

Until about three weeks later, when he showed up at my house to keep me company while I was stuck in bed. He had brought me a get-well-soon present. *Wings Greatest*. I had no idea he knew music was my "thing," and I remember being so touched by how attentive my friend was. Music definitely wasn't his thing. I'm not sure what his thing was, but judging by his preferred after-school activities and his affinity for vehicular speed, I'm assuming adrenaline was his thing.

But I remember feeling truly uplifted and "seen," as we say today. It just felt so completely perfect and not accidental. It wasn't a wild guess. He had thought about it. And his thoughtfulness had led him to a truly personal gift for his laid-up friend. I mean, compared to the jigsaw puzzles and stuffed animals ("For the thousandth time, I'm allergic to dust, people!") from my relatives, you'd think this kid was the closest friend I ever had. But he wasn't. He was just a sweetheart who cared about people enough to listen to them when they talked about things he wasn't as interested in. You know, a good person.

We never really crossed paths again. I think he moved and ended up at a different school. But I think about him every time I hear "Mull of Kintyre" and how great it felt to have someone see me the way I was just beginning to see myself. Especially at a moment in my life where my true identity felt so hidden and invisible to others. And I'm also always reminded to keep working on my ability to pay attention to people in a way that would lead me to their *Wings Greatest* if they ever needed some warmhearted cheering up. It's a good way to be.

LOUD, LOUD, LOUD

IF YOU'VE EVER WONDERED WHAT A MANSON FAMILY—led community theater troupe would sound like rehearsing a copyright-avoiding knockoff mash-up of *Hair* and *Jesus Christ Superstar* (let's call it *Jesus Hair*), I think I have some good news for you.

Aphrodite's Child's *666* is your ticket. I think it's just about the wildest, most over-the-top, one-of-a-kind, and insane rock concept album ever made. The audacious conceits and pretensions of the Who's *Tommy* sound perfectly reasonable by comparison. "They should've called it *Timmy*," I said to myself once, deep in the throes of *666* reverie.

The album was recorded in late 1970 and early 1971 by Vangelis and a crazy cast of Greek luminaries (including Irene Papas) that apparently disbanded before the album was finally released in 1972. The lyrics are supposedly based on the Book of Revelation. And I'm sorry, but that's the best I've ever been able to muster by way of offering up a coherent synopsis. I can tell you it's one of my favorite albums of all time and my physical copy is one of my most prized possessions.

So how did I end up with this tortured slab of surreal (Dalí was a fan!) European counterculture prog? Well . . . have you ever heard of cargo cults? Those remote uncontacted groups living on islands in the Pacific that would form societies and religions around the mysterious items that would wash up on their beaches? Most often these items had been provided by "sky gods" (i.e., planes)— miscalculated supply drops and downed aircraft and equipment from as early as World War II. Yes, it's a stretch, but I totally relate to how something like that could work. Because although I grew up solidly middle-class in an American small town with access to the world through televisions and phones and a relatively modern existence, I have to say I know what it feels like to have something incomprehensible practically land on my head: a full crate of my older brother's mysterious and eclectic record collection. Gifted to me in exchange for a promise to never order records from the Columbia House record club.

In 1976, these felt like the kinds of records no other nine-year-old in the world would have been (or should have been) listening to. LPs by Amon Düül II, Kraftwerk, and Tangerine Dream, to name just a few. And, of course, 666, the subject of this piece. Now, almost fifty years later, it's still a pretty adventurous cross-section of recorded history. And I didn't just own them, I LIS-TENED to them. I learned them. I formed an internal culture warped by the cosmic experiment of giving an anomalous set of references to an unworldly though curious musical mind. (I always think that these records, combined with my aunt's and my older sister's [also inherited] Monkees and Motown seven-inch records, succinctly explain almost every musical move I've ever made.)

As a way to honor this bountiful box—this seeming Rosetta stone to a language I had no idea had never been spoken—I could have picked a number of songs off this album as representative. Like "The System," with its simultaneously naughty and invigorating (to a nine-year-old) chorus, "We got the system to FUCK the system!"

But this is the song I've returned to the most.

"Loud, Loud, Loud."

Let me set the scene. In your mind's eye (ear?), picture these lyrics spoken by the most painfully earnest young woman's voice you can imagine (I used to always picture Manson-ite Patricia Krenwinkel reciting these words before I learned through researching this book that it's actually Daniel Koplowitz, the young son of a diplomat) over what sounds like someone learning how to alternate between two simple chords on a piano.

The day the walls of the cities will crumble away
Uncovering our naked souls

We'll all start singing . . .
Shouting . . .
Screaming . . .

A chorus of unmistakably dissociated voices joins in with a four-note descending chant.

Loud, loud, loud, loud

You can almost hear the matching tracksuits.

The day the circus horses will stop turning around
Running fast through the green valleys
We'll sing . . .
And cry . . .
And shout . . .
Loud, loud, loud, loud

We're marching into the flames now, people. Eyes fixed on the smoldering horizon . . .

The day the cars will lay in heaps
Their wheels turning in vain
We'll run along the empty highways
Shouting . . .
Screaming . . .
Singing . . .

Chorus getting . . . um . . . louder now . . .

Loud, loud, loud, loud
The day young boys will stop becoming soldiers
And soldiers will stop playing war games
We'll sing and cry and shout

Tension building . . .

Loud, LOUD, LOUD, LOUD
The day will come up
That we'll all wake up

Yes! That's how powerful this song is. Not every song can take a hit like rhyming *up* with *up*.

Hearing the shout of joy
And shouting together with the freaks

This word "freaks." I had no business identifying with this word as a nine-year-old. And I probably shouldn't claim it now. But the heart knows what the heart knows.

And it continues . . .

The day the world will turn upside down
We'll run together 'round and 'round
Screaming . . .

Shouting . . .
Singing . . .

Still escalating . . .

Loud, loud, loud, loud
Loud, loud, loud, loud
Loud, loud, loud, loud

Is this song silly? Undeniably. Do I still get goose bumps? Every single time. And I think that's the point worth making here. I don't think you should ever override what your body is telling you about a song. Life's too short to let your critical thinking get in the way of being moved by music. I mean, what's more important? Catharsis? Or feeling intellectually superior to someone else's art?

By the way, on the album this song cross-fades into Demis Roussos's unmistakable hornlike voice singing the opening lyrics of "The Four Horsemen." And if you're listening to these tracks along with the book, I highly recommend continuing through this song as well and treating yourself to possibly (at the proper volume) the most exciting drum fills ever recorded.

Fuck yeah!

OLIVER GOTHIC

WHEN I WAS AROUND NINE YEARS OLD MY MOTHER read about something called "Tree House Camp" in the local paper, noticed that it was very close to where she worked, and enrolled me for the upcoming summer "session."

The picture in the ad looked like it might have been a still from *Swiss Family Robinson*. The elaborate wooden chalets and walkways between them, all suspended in some type of forest canopy that looked like none of the wooded areas I'd ever seen in my neck of the . . . um, wooded areas . . . did raise some suspicion. Something about it reminded me of the disgusting jar of briny water that sat on my bookshelf, the one that was clearly never going to transform into an adorable family of "Sea-Monkeys."

But like any kid my age, the dream of inhabiting a space among the squirrels and birds, separate from, and above, the ground-dwelling adults—it was all intoxicating and drowned out any alarm bells that my (and I'm assuming my mother's) better judgment should have set off.

We arrived the morning of the first day at a fallow field on the outskirts of town—overgrown but decidedly flat and treeless. My mother, who I'm sure was late for work and had very much intended to drop me off with little more than what you would call a rolling stop, decided she needed to park the car, get out, and ask someone the question that was on both of our minds:

"Where are the fucking trees!?"

"See over there? Them trees popping up just beyond the horizon? That's where the camp is. We own all this land but this here spot is the closest we can get a car for dropping off the kids."

"Ah, okay," my mother said, nodding, "makes sense."

"Does it?" I thought as we began the long walk through the weeds and I watched my mother's car disappear over my shoulder. As she waited for a break in the traffic to pull out, I was quickly calculating if the distance I'd walked so far was already past the point of no return, alongside how furious she'd be if I bailed. Too late. As she made it out onto the road, she looked back, saw me looking at her, and gave a chipper little toot on her horn that I found unconvincing. I knew I was doomed.

"First thing we gotta do is clear this brush . . . ," said

the dour, sun-dried, semi-toothed, drifter-type gentle-
man handing me a machete, "so we can get up to them
trees and start to buildin'."

By mid-June, when this was all happening, the
heat and humidity in southern Illinois is brutal, even in
the morning. Inhospitable. Even to a dumb kid who
was decades away from being softened by central air-
conditioning. Which, by the way, was a topic I often
heard my folks discussing as something they would be
able to afford once I got a job and left the house or went
away to college. Again, I was nine.

So I definitely remember being way too hot. But the
rest of my memory of this episode is muddy. And, although it has the distinct weight and knurled texture I
associate with trauma, I have almost zero direct images
attached to this short chapter in my life beyond the ini-
tial drop-off and my preteen mental confirmation of a
swindle.

Basically, the con was to get a bunch of kids to clear
some land. Kind of ingenious, really. Diabolical even.
And when you consider the fact that they had charged
our parents for our services as opposed to . . . oh, I don't
know . . . PAYING ANYTHING AT ALL, you begin
to clearly see some real Mark Twain–type scoundrels. I
mean, if you weren't around in the midseventies, let me
tell you, kids my age would mow a football-field-sized
lawn with a push mower for a couple of bucks. Happily!

So, again, the people who concocted this whole scheme were some grade-A sociopaths.

Oddly, I also don't remember much about the other kids. I don't think there were many of us. I have a vague memory of us all mirthlessly holding our implements: hoes, rakes, shovels, hatchets, saws, machetes, and scythes, like the cast of *Oliver!* crossed with *American Gothic*.

What I do remember is that this was the last time my mother ever made an effort to push me out of the nest. I know she felt bad when she picked me up, sunburned and angry, later that afternoon.

So I ended up going to work with my mother a lot that summer. She worked at a cabinet place and I'd spend the day pretending I lived in the display kitchens and bathrooms. Sometimes I'd climb around on the massive rolls of carpeting in the warehouse. But that activity usually ended with my eyes burning and itching, watering, turning red, and sometimes even swelling shut. Mom said it was the chemicals they sprayed on the carpeting to make it "safe." She thought I might be allergic to them, because it didn't bother her. But I also didn't see her rolling around on them.

When we would leave to go home that summer, my mom would often swing by the site of the "Tree House Camp" just to see what kind of fun I might be missing and if there were any actual tree houses being built.

We never saw any.

BOTH SIDES NOW

THERE ARE SOME SONGS SO PERFECT IT'S IMPOSSIBLE to imagine them ever not existing. Melodies so seamless that it makes no sense to contemplate how they were constructed. Miniature suns and moons. Here long before us, and sure to survive long after we're gone. Music that arrives not as something new but as something that finally has a name. This song feels like it's been a part of me for as long as I've had a me to feel.

It seems certain that I must have heard this song as an infant. Judy Collins's version was riding high on the charts shortly after my first birthday, so it's not unlikely that it would have seeped into my consciousness around the same exact time my developing mind's language centers were just kicking into gear. If that's the explanation for this feeling I have that this song is purely a geological fact, then lucky me. What a gift it's been to have this song on speed dial my entire life. I can't always remember all the words, but the melody is always there. It almost feels like it has a specific physical presence. With its own unique feeling. Like a grade school locker-lined hallway. Or maybe it's more like a loved one's face. Like how I can close my eyes and see my sister as a young woman getting married, then later, smiling beneath silver-gray bangs. Like how both those images ARE my sister to me, wherever I am in the world.

It's love that I'm describing, isn't it? I trust this song so much. Its wisdom, lyrically, is astonishing. And as simple as it may sound, "Something's lost, but something's gained / In living every day," when combined with such an indelible melody, is a pretty remarkable bit of consolation to have coming out of your radio. And, in turn, on a loop in your head for more than fifty years. How? Joni Mitchell was barely out of her teens when she wrote this song. So again I ask, how? Pure magic. Pure genius.

If somehow you aren't familiar with this song, please go listen to it now if you can. Trust me, you need it. And if it doesn't keep you company for a long time, I hope you have a song that feels, to you, the way I've described this one. I'd be lost without it.

So . . . It's a good thing it can't be taken away from me. Not even if I never heard it again. It is a part of the world I live in. Like air and water.

8

LUCKY NUMBER

GROWING UP BEING MY MOM'S BEST FRIEND HAD some perks. She was a night owl. Liked watching old movies and didn't particularly care if I ever went to bed as long as I got up in the morning to go to school. With hindsight it's now clear that some boundary-setting and better sleep hygiene would have saved me a fortune in counseling. But if that had been the case, who knows where I'd be. Happier? Who's to say. I do know that I probably would have never been exposed to some great Judy Garland and Mickey Rooney movies without that loose structure.

And if had kept normal kid hours in 1979, there's a good chance I would have missed one of the most important television events of my lifetime: the all–"New Wave" episode of *The Midnight Special*. First of all, where I grew up in southern Illinois we watched St. Louis TV stations, and the "Midnight" part of *The Midnight*

Special meant two A.M. on either Friday or Saturday night. That's how low in the programming hierarchy this syndicated music program was. They didn't even feel like they had to honor the time advertised right there in the title.

Mom usually controlled the clicker (actually I'm pretty sure we didn't have a TV remote yet—point is, we watched what she wanted to watch as a rule), but she was pretty good about letting me watch music programs because she knew how much they meant to me. To be honest, these shows were usually kind of a drag; I hated about 75 percent of the acts they'd have on. Pablo Cruise on *Don Kirshner's Rock Concert*? No thank you! I'm twelve. Cocaine, I know not what it is. But something is making you all look like my grandmother's standard poodle in need of a walk.

Not on this night, though. Check out this lineup— the Cars! (live), Suicide! (doing "Dream Baby Dream" and "Ghost Rider" LIVE!), the Records (meh), and Iggy Pop ("Five Foot One" and "I'm Bored"!), along with clips by M ("Pop Muzik," a 45 rpm I bought with my own money) and Lene Lovich doing "Say When" and "Lucky Number."

That's a big night for a kid looking for anything that can match the weirdness and excitement of the odd "cargo cult" crate of records stashed away in his bedroom. I wanted mind-warping stuff. It's what I had unreasonably come to expect for my entertainment dollar. I could probably make an equally compelling case for almost any of the songs I heard that night for the first time (minus the Records' set).

They all made indelible impressions, but I think Lene Lovich's song "Lucky Number" still feels like the most poignant reminder of that late night to me. More so because of my mother's reaction than my own. She lit up at Lene's eccentricity. Something about the combination of her old-world costume and bizarre modern mannerisms got my drowsy mother to sit up and pay attention in a way none of the male-dominated acts had achieved.

"She's different," was her assessment on the whole. "Lucky Number" was the bigger hit in my mother's estimation of Lovich's two songs. She liked it so much that she helped me find the record at Venture that weekend. Miraculously, we found a copy of Lovich's debut album, *Stateless*. To be honest, this reaction and strong endorsement of such a weird performer puzzled me a bit at the time. I loved the song because it was exciting and bold music with odd angular melodic jumps that felt almost like another song from some other dimension was periodically interrupting, like an impatient kid in the lunch line at school, jumping ahead to grab the last slice of pizza.

In hindsight, the reasons for my mother's apparent affinity for this particular tune have become much more obvious to me. My mother often offered up this bit of tragic advice to me: "You're born alone and you'll die alone, so you might as well get used to being alone." She was a brilliant woman, but this is obviously a grim outlook on life that someone with a bit more awareness of healthy boundaries would have kept a million miles away from a sensitive young lad like myself. It made me sad then. And it still makes me sad, knowing how born of experience that aphorism must have been for my mom. And in some way, I'm sure, protecting herself with this shield of bullshit must have helped keep her sane.

But on this night more than forty years ago, I watched her hear someone else sing "My lucky number is ONE." I saw it with my own eyes. She lit up at the idea that someone else, even someone as weird as Lene Lovich, could understand where she was coming from. My mom heard herself. I'm sure of it now. And it makes me happy to know that whether she made the connection or not, in that moment she was not alone. She never was.

HAT-WEARING KIND OF GUY

NOTICING THAT MY LOUD, DRUNK FRIEND HAD GONE uncharacteristically silent while cutting my hair, after I'd been talked into a rattail at his insistence. My eyes focusing on a bedroom dresser mirror one room across from the kitchen table where I sat, as it slowly dawned on me that his mute status was due to a violent laughing fit that had bent him over against the wall, gasping for air, as he surveyed his handiwork. He had unilaterally decided my hair wasn't quite long enough for a satisfying rattail, so he had elected to shave upward toward the tops of my ears on either side of my scalp. Giving me what looked like the haircut equivalent of a coonskin cap. Summer school began the following day.

. . . I've always been a hat-wearing kind of guy.

9

GLORIA

"JESUS DIED FOR SOMEBODY'S SINS BUT NOT MINE."

Has there ever been a more attention-grabbing first line of a record? Patti Smith's album *Horses* was yet another providence-delivered document slipped under the door of the mental cage that was late-seventies small-town life, via my brother's gifted stash.

Hearing these words in the environment I lived in, at the age I heard them, felt dangerous. Without exaggeration. I was born a skeptic. And my suspicion of organized religion grew as I grew. It's hard to describe the innate revulsion the idea of going to church instilled in me. Witnessing a couple of my cousins transform from being totally fun to be around to absolutely terrifying monomaniacal Jesus freaks didn't help with the paranoia.

Religion was something I feared catching like a flu. Or being bit by a vampire bat. I had no idea how to

protect myself from what appeared to be such an ir-
rational mindset befalling me. How did it happen? Was
marijuana (which I had a vague awareness of, courtesy of
these same slightly older relatives) truly a gateway drug?
I had no idea how to remain vigilant, except to reaffirm
to myself on a regular basis that things did not add up. I
remember thinking to myself, "If Jesus is so great, why
are you (a person who I used to really like) such a pain
in the ass to be around?"

Luckily, my mom and dad were decidedly lax about
churchgoing. Easter? You bet. Christmas? Midnight
mass seems like a long shot. Let's play it by ear and keep
tabs on Dad's beer intake. And that was about it. That is,
until I reached confirmation age. For some reason they
insisted I start going to Sunday school and studying to
be confirmed. With the welcome caveat that if I finished
my confirmation and took communion, I could then
choose whether or not I ever stepped foot in church
again.

St. Paul United Church of Christ was the congrega-
tion they had both attended since they were kids. It was
the chapel where I had been christened. So in theory, I
understood the request. In practice, it was painful.

Before I get too far ahead of myself, let me say I'm as
confused as you are about the denomination. People
would always ask me what denomination I was growing
up. And I'd say, "Christian." And they'd go, "Duh!
What kind of Christian?" And I'd say, "Ummm . . . the

United Church of kind?" To which they might reply, "But I thought you were going to take communion. Aren't you Catholic then?" And I'd say, "Ever since my sister had holy water thrown on her at a sleepover and came home scared she was going to hell, my mom has been pretty negative about Catholics, so I don't think that's it."

The truth is, my mom came by her own religious skepticism the good old-fashioned way. Growing up, her bedroom window was situated directly behind a convent and a seminary. She always claimed the traffic between the two—the trysts and the general sneaking around— kept her awake at night. "They're all a bunch of phonies," she'd say. But I only heard these stories later. At the time we're talking about, she was biting her tongue, determined not to put her finger on the scale of my salvation, I guess. Of course, my true salvation was one no one could save me from. Mostly because they had no better chance of understanding my deliverance from the dark than I had of understanding theirs. I've often heard Patti Smith described as a punk priestess. Which leads me to believe that I'm not alone in marking my first introduction to her voice as a rapturous event. A conversion of sorts. I already had a passion for music. But until I heard this song (and the thirty-five minutes or so of rock that followed), I'm not sure I understood catharsis or the terrifyingly transformative power an individual performer can possess. Every line of lyric a shard of poetry sung with the spirit and cadence of a taunt. Whatcha gonna do about it?!

> *Thick heart of stone*
> *My sins my own*
> *They belong to me, ME*

God, how I dreamed about one day standing up for myself, unafraid of not fitting in. I still dream of possessing Patti's fearlessness, but that's beside the point. I needed this music. I'm lucky it found me at such an early age. Any later might have been too late. Some might describe this event as divine intervention. It's a concept that is hard to argue with.

AS IF IT ALWAYS
HAPPENS

SLOVENLY WAS A BAND ON SST RECORDS. SST, IF YOU
don't know, was an independent punk rock record label.
In fact, it was probably the first non-major label any of
us kids walking around calling ourselves "punks" in the
early eighties had ever really heard of. In the truest spirit
of DIY, Black Flag founding guitarist Greg Ginn repurposed the company he had started when he was twelve
to sell homemade ham-radio electronics (SST stands for
Solid State Tuners) into a record label so the band could
put out their own music. And they quickly realized that
a lot of their less enterprising and not as "together"
friends could use some help getting their records out, too.

And as it turned out, pretty much all of their friends
had something incredible to share with the world, musically. For a while, it felt like every record I bought was on
SST, and everything I listened to influenced my own
music. Minutemen! All-timers. Meat Puppets! Where

would I be without them? Hüsker Dü! Um, have you ever heard Uncle Tupelo? On and on it continued . . . Sonic Youth, Dinosaur Jr., all extremely important records. Not just to me. Whether you're aware of it or not, these are the records that shaped a lot of your favorite bands.

Sounds like hyperbole. It's not. Tell me some of your favorite records and I feel confident I could draw a direct connection to at least one SST release. The label had a batting average so high my friends and I started doing something we'd never even considered before—buying records by bands we'd never heard of based only on SST's ostensibly liking them enough to put their record out. We had all rolled the dice based on a cool album cover, sure . . . and it wasn't unheard of to hand over some cash based on a terrific band name (Butthole Surfers comes to mind). It seemed absurd to buy a record only because it was on a label like Columbia or Warner Bros., but SST felt so deeply curated and reliable that we all ended up being the kind of record consumer who would scour the bins flipping records over, looking for their logo.

I keep saying "we" because I want it to be known that as I've gotten older and traveled around, and met more and more musicians, I've come to understand that what initially felt like a unique personality trait was in reality something I had in common with way more people than I would have ever been able to understand in those pre-internet days. I was perfectly normal back in my early teens, albeit a little lonely and obsessed. Would have been nice to know that back then, but an equally likely guess is that it might have destroyed me to feel a little less special.

One of the ways I could have figured out how much I had in common with others might have been by understanding the principles of marketing, even just a little bit. Because when SST began negating the need to hunt for their imprint by affixing stickers emblazoned with their logo to their shrink-wrapped front covers, the writing really was on the wall. My reaction at the time was devoid of suspicion. It saved me time. I kept buying pretty much anything they put out.

And then, the laws of free-market capitalism began to be applied. It seemed like the more SST records I bought, the more they would release. Eventually it was financially impossible to keep up. So I was forced to regain a more scrutinizing style of buying records. Not before I found myself owning decidedly less classic albums, by the likes of Lawndale and Zoogz Rift. Fun records to own. I still have them. But let's just say they're nonessential.

So where am I going with all of this indie label lore? Slovenly. That's where I'm heading. SST put out their album *Riposte (a Little Resolve)* right in the middle of my SST spending spree. And to a lot of people, most of my friends included, this record landed somewhere on the downward slope of our ability to trust quality to the logo alone. Not me, though. I have listened to this record as much as almost any other record I own. I get that the singing, especially, wasn't an easy sell for a lot of people. Ian Curtis by way of California isn't far off.

But for me, this record sums up my feelings and affinity for do-it-yourself beauty. In essence, this song is an ecstatic poem about an epiphanous moment in the park—"Being with all of those . . . BAAAY-BIES"— read over some uniquely latticed post-punk guitars. It weaves and swoons. Stops abruptly like a hand slapping a desk and resumes with a sigh.

This is aspirational art. Aimed squarely at catharsis. There is no reason for this music to exist outside of those very lofty goals. This music aims at a purpose high above commerce, popularity . . . I can hardly bring myself to say stardom. It's unabashed in its artistic ambition. It's a few people of similar ages and mindsets—friends— allowing themselves to be vulnerable as a collective. Without much promised in the way of reward, other than to have some music to listen to that no one else could make but them. The ultimate dream for me, ever since this record taught me to dream in this way. With my friends. In whichever direction we choose.

TERRY

THE ONLY BONA FIDE FIRST-WAVE PUNK ROCKER IN my hometown of Belleville, Illinois—a man we'll just refer to as Terry—insisting to a teen me that "noise music" is the only thing worth listening to. Teen me mail-ordering Psyclones' *Cult Leader Gang-Raped by Disciples* cassette-only release—featuring a man having his mouth forcibly opened and pissed in on the hand-folded cardboard insert cover. Dropping news of my recent purchase into some casual record store counter conversation mere weeks later, where Terry vehemently denounces "noise music"—"Noise music is fraud, man. POP music is all I listen to. But not like the Beatles! The Monkees, MAN! The Beatles are pretentious bullshit. Monkees are pure pop! Noise is over. You gotta get into POP!"

Teen me realizing Terry is a dangerous person.

SOMEWHERE OVER
THE RAINBOW

WHEN I WAS GROWING UP, AROUND SEVEN OR EIGHT years old, I thought I knew the Cowardly Lion. Better yet, I thought my sister was going to get engaged to him, and I remember being giddy at the thought of having such an esteemed family member.

I admired my sister for being able to land such a big fish. But it turned out he was just a local actor who had played the part a few times in a local repertory theater and liked doing his best Bert Lahr impression for impressionable little kids. The dream really fell apart when I was dragged to see him perform as Willy Loman in *Death of a Salesman* at a St. Louis dinner theater, IN THE ROUND. Not long after, he and my sister broke it off. He went on to star in a pretty major ad campaign for Burger King as a character they had created named Herb. Researching it, it appears that there were several Herbs, separated by regional markets. The bit was based

on the slogan "Where's Herb?" He'd be in local com-
mercials as Herb and then they'd send him out to cause
a stir by showing up at Burger Kings around the Midwest. It was a simpler time. Still, he and my sister remained on good terms, so we were all proud of him.

It's a strange memory to associate with something so
sublime, but that's the truth of where my mind goes
when I hear "Somewhere over the Rainbow." I always
think of "Herb," or "what's his name," as my dad
called him.

And then I think of my mother. Sitting up on the
couch with me very late in the night, watching Judy
Garland movies in our pajamas. My mother watching
Judy sing. Me watching my mom, through the TV-lit
blue twists and curls of her cigarette smoke, become as
soft as a child, mouthing along silently, eyes wide, fully
transported. Loving her so much and being so happy to
see her look so different, knowing even at that age how
important it was for her to get to be somewhere else, if
only for a moment.

It's as perfect a memory as I have of my mother, and
it's a perfect song. No one will ever write one better.

DEATH OR GLORY

THERE WAS A BRIEF PERIOD IN THE EARLY EIGHTIES when the older of my two brothers lived in a small but nice apartment on the Upper West Side of Manhattan with his wife at the time. I won't go into the details of how that came to be. Because I don't really remember them. But it had something to do with his wife being on an executive fast track with some big-time accounting firm. My first-ever introduction to New York City was when my mom and I went to visit them. We got the typical tourist impressions at the time. Central Park is wonderful. Subways are loud. And holy shit, I've never seen so many people in my life.

But the thing about that trip that left the deepest, most indelible mark on me was seeing street musicians for the first time. Violinists, steel drummers, classical guitarists, pianists, everywhere. In the park, in the subway, ON the subway cars. To me, a super-curious,

budding romantic artist type, it was exhilarating witnessing people laying out their hats and guitar cases to
collect coins and the occasional paper money. "I see"—
jotting down a mental note—"they appear to be paying
their dues."

But the intimidating part, the part I've thought
about a lot since that first encounter with the largeness
of everything, is that those same musicians also indi-
rectly informed me of my own smallness. They were all
so good. Invariably, my mom and I would walk away
shaking our heads in disbelief at the musicianship we'd
just witnessed. Just astonished at there being so much
talent, and then thinking if this is just what the street
has to offer, what on earth are they doing in places like
Carnegie Hall? It was uplifting, because it's always uplifting to be in the presence of an artist being great at
what they do. But boy, did it hammer home how bad I
sucked at the guitar.

Another takeaway—a realization that must have
been subliminally received at my mother's side in the
eighties, a bit of wisdom about how the world operates
that has slowly been working its way toward the front of
my brain for decades now until this very moment—is
how invulnerable all the musicians were. They dressed
how they pleased and poured their hearts out in the
public square. Where I grew up, both of those traits could
get you a solid beating, or at the very least a healthy dose
of merciless ridicule. It wouldn't have mattered how good

you were at your flute, jackass. How were they unafraid and safe from that ugliness? I wanted to feel like that. Where does one sign up for that kind of moxie, I wondered. The answer is the city. The city has the power to inoculate one against judgment. The bigger the better. Everyone's busy. Everyone has seen it all. The more people there are, the less power any one group has to shame people into the shadows.

So what did this subtle transmission communicate to this wide-eyed sponge on a cellular level? I asked my mom if she would buy me a beret. And she did. She even told me repeatedly how much she loved it when I wore it the rest of the trip. I felt bold in it. More myself. Or at least, wearing a beret made me feel like a person I had a hand in inventing.

It felt good. It didn't last. I have a vivid memory from when I got back home of having my beret on, hopping out of my mom's car after getting dropped off at school, then realizing within seconds the catastrophic miscalculation I was making, blithely ambling into a buzz saw of humiliation. Then, in one swift motion, wiping that ridiculous round puff of felt off the top of my head and into my bag. It didn't happen if no one saw it. Death or glory indeed!

So what does this have to do with "Death or Glory" the song—how do the Clash figure into this biographical miniature? Well, aside from the fact that the only reason I could have possibly wanted a beret was because

I saw the Clash wearing them, I think this story is kind of at the very core of who I am. It illustrates the still-constant battle I have between the learned suspicion of my own desire to feel liberated and my deep natural need to actively create, not just works of art but who I am, through discovery by way of trial and error.

If you've ever seen me perform, I'm sure it's obvious that every time I walk up to the edge of showmanship I say something stupid like, "As far as audiences go, you guys are okay. And that's saying something because I don't really like audiences. In fact, statistically there are only about three or four of you I'd want to hang out with." That's the internal seesawing at work. That's Belleville Jeff jumping in and interrupting Beret Jeff. "Imma let you finish, but berets make you look like a pretentious acorn."

The Clash symbolizes all of this to me more than any other band I've loved. They make me cringe. I cringe at wanting to be them. But I still love them. Like family. They made me who I am, but that's not all as lovely as it might imply.

SCHADENFREUDE
BUFFET

WHEN I WAS GROWING UP, EACH MEMBER OF MY family absolutely detested their counterpart in our next-door neighbors' family. The Winkers. My mom avoided the mom. Dad thought the dad was a phony. My brothers had a beef with the son. And the daughter was my nemesis. No idea what happened to make it so. It just was, and everyone accepted that we hated each other.

Every once in a while there would be some thawing of relations. A detente. Christmastime seemed to put everyone on their best behavior, for example. Never lasted long. One day, shortly after Christmas 1978, Rufus, the oldest son, whom my parents only ever referred to as "Dufus" (us being a unified front when it came to talking shit about the Winkers), was pacing around in their backyard talking into some kind of walkie-talkie, looking up at the sky. My dad pulls up in the driveway that divided our two backyards. Home from work, gets out of his "company" car. Sees Rufus acting weird and shouts over at him, "Whatcha up to, Ruf?"

"I got this for Christmas. Trying to talk to an airplane," he replies, still staring at the clouds.

"Ah. That's neat. Good luck!"

Dad comes in the back door and heads straight downstairs to his TV workshop in the corner of the basement (he taught himself TV repair as a side hustle in the early sixties). Which just happens to have a ham radio and a small window with a good, slightly hidden view of the Winkers' backyard. And Rufus. After cracking open a fresh beer, Dad calls me downstairs. And after some dial twirling, he finally latches on to Rufus's frequency and begins a conversation—in the dead-bored, matter-of-fact, jargon-y style of an ex-military airline pilot. "Comin' in loud and clear . . . *KRRCHK* . . . what's your twenty . . . *KRRCHK* . . . TWA eighteen fifty-five . . . *KRRCHK* . . . outbound Wichita . . . *KRRCHK* . . . over . . . *KRRCHK*."

My dad sipping on his beer in the dark with me watching Rufus excitedly running around in circles shouting his name and home address into his handset. Tickled, and trying to contain his own glee, Dad growls at me, "Stop giggling, boy! Now watch this . . . *KRRCHK* . . . Ten-four. Hello, Rufus Winker of Illinois! . . . *KRRCHK* . . . TWA eighteen fifty-five . . . *KRRCHK* . . . We'll be back overhead—inbound at nineteen hundred hours . . . *KRRCHK* . . . gather up some flashlights and shine 'em up at the sky and I'll fly by real low and flash my emergency lights . . . *KRRCHK*."

Seven thirty P.M. CST, casually walking outside with Mom and Dad to ask the Winkers "what the hell are you up to now with them goddamn flashlights?!" Just as their arms were growing heavy and their frustration was starting to boil over, laying bare delicious internal cracks, fissures, and flaws. As they were starting to snipe at each other. Ol' Rufus getting derided from all sides. A veritable schadenfreude buffet.

Might be the closest I ever felt to my mom and dad at the same time. I hate that we bonded over something so mean. I'll take it. But I wish there was more. I hate that there wasn't.

To any surviving Winkers out there, I'd like to say I'm sorry. I'm sure you had your issues, but I'm pretty sure we were the bad guys. In this case at the very least. Love and peace.

MY SHARONA

LET'S TALK ABOUT ROCK JOURNALISM FOR A BIT. I like it. I even love some of it. But before I offer up my deeper thoughts on the topic, a caveat directed toward any practitioners of this dark art who might be reading must be stated. Actually, two caveats. I have dual caveats.

First: I'm aware that I am forever indebted to you all for the travail—the shitty pay, the late nights, the stressful deadlines, the long hours. No doubt they have taken their toll on many of you. We share a passion, and without your diligence I'm sure there are countless bands and records I would never have stumbled upon. Thank you.

Second: I'm likewise conscious of the fact that in the grand scheme of things, the bands I've been in and the records I've made, by and large, have been welcomed into the world with a remarkably low level of rancor. Especially considering my reluctance to stop making records and being in bands. There have even been points along the way where I've seen the adorable (and financially chilling) phrase "critics' darling" directed my way. It's been a good run. Nothing I'm about to say should in any way register as complaint.

Okay, one more caveat. (With the caveat that three—now four—caveats is too many caveats. *Yoda voice* Slippery slope, caveats are.) I get that writing about songs and records is technically some form of music journalism we're engaging in here. But I'm really trying to avoid the critic part of that equation (with the exception of Bon Jovi; fuck—another caveat) because that's the problem with music writing; it's the critiquing part, right? The weighing of one against the other, the numbering, the grading, the weird arrogance of forming an opinion, writing it down, and then also giving grades or awarding stars. In effect saying, "Hey, everybody, I wrote a thousand words about the new Crystal Ümlauts LP" (made-up band name) "but if you're in a hurry it's three stars. You know, it's okay, nothing to write home about." It's an odd practice that takes the pretense of writing about art with academic seriousness—dissecting, parsing language, important contextualizing of cultural discourse—then walks it all the way up to the altar and chickens out. "What the hell was I thinking, no one's going to read this shit, ugh . . . here, here's a number, it means it's pretty good. You like music? Well, this is music. It's . . . okay."

I guess it makes sense that music journalism has a tough time getting its story straight about how seriously it wants to be taken. Because let's face it, the idea that what makes music so important at its core could be critiqued and rated is laughable in the face of the genuine promise almost any record can deliver to the listener. A promise that says, "I am here. Sing with me. Out loud or to yourself. I will always be here when you need me, you are not alone." Songs are our companions. Some become friends for life, but any song in the air has the potential to keep you company for a little while. The way you might form a brief bond with someone in the checkout line. Rock 'n' roll is doubly insulated from the indignities of being assayed by the mind alone. By my definition, rock 'n' roll is anything that can be itself without thinking or fear of consequence. Best friend material in my book. It's music made by bored teenagers, maladjusted adults, and most important, inspired amateurs.

Great rock 'n' roll can be, and often is, much better than the people making it. A lot of times it happens in spite of the contrivances surrounding its genesis. It's magic that can be conjured almost anywhere by almost anyone. Because we as listeners get a say, too. We can make something truly rock 'n' roll just by hearing it with a pure heart. There's no point in arguing about it. Which is why it was so confusing for me as a kid to see so much critical vitriol heaped on the Knack's first record. Not that they weren't right in the long run. The band did have reprehensible lyrics. There were contrivances. But boy did that shit sound stupid when "My Sharona" came on the radio. Totally undeniable rock miracle. It stirred something in me in 1979 that has yet to come to rest.

At twelve years old, I didn't have a lot of friends who could hang with my obsessive level of rock zealotry. So again, as we've seen in previous chapters, that left only my mom to talk to. Fortunately for me, she was able to be a genuinely patient and indulging listener. She'd smile and nod. Obviously bemused to see her often withdrawn and quiet kid enthusiastic about anything.

So we're in the drive-thru at McDonald's. I'd already heard "My Sharona" a few times by now. And as I was getting worked up trying to explain how great it was to my mom, it came on the radio. Unbelievable timing. Now, for those of you who don't remember, there were two versions—one was a radio edit for the shorter song format of AM pop radio, and then there was the longer album version that the more freewheeling FM stations would play. I was so excited that we were listening to KSHE, because that meant that the extended middle section of the song would be intact. The part of the song I had just breathlessly proclaimed to my mother to be the hardest of all the rocking I had ever heard. Pointing out that the rocking gets so hard and strenuous that at one point you can actually hear the musicians breathing heavily.

"Oh wow," she says as we pull up to the pickup

window. "Here it is!" I say as I crank the volume. Now my mother is reaching to grab a bag containing my Filet-O-Fish and fries from a frightened cashier as Doug Fieger climaxes to the beat blowing out the dash speakers of my mom's Caprice Classic. As we slowly move back into traffic, she calmly rolls her window back up and turns the radio down. The color of her face foreshadowing the lessons of a health class unit I had heard about but had yet to be taught. And I arrived at the conclusion that I would prefer to always think of the panting-and-heaving section of "My Sharona" the way I had originally interpreted it.

IN GERMANY BEFORE THE WAR

IT'S HARD TO BELIEVE A SONG LIKE THIS COULD POS-sibly coexist on the same album with a song like "Short People." Much less on the same side—but there they are, bookending side one on Randy Newman's 1977 album *Little Criminals*. Wanna know something else hard to believe? "Short People" was a massive hit. It would have even made it to number one on the *Billboard* charts if it weren't for "Baby Come Back" by Player. Oh, that and another little song called "STAYIN' ALIVE" by the Bee Gees. I'm guessing number two still feels pretty great, though, when the song above yours is a cultural phenomenon, not to mention an unstoppable juggernaut of record sales.

I, like most people, bought *Little Criminals* for "Short People." Which at the time was sort of controversial. Because a lot of people were dumb and couldn't understand the idea that a singer could sing something they themselves didn't believe. I knew it was a song about prejudice, and I was ten. It wasn't Randy Newman's fault people were laughing at the wrong joke, but I'm sure it sucked to be a little person in 1978 when this song was a close-to-unavoidable part of daily life. This is the kind of thing people like to point to and say stuff like, "There's no way you could get away with a song like that today," and usually I think to myself that they're being small-minded dopes.

But in this case, I think they have a point. Randy Newman himself would probably think better of rolling the dice with a song as mean-spirited as this one today. You can tell people all day long that your lyrics are sung from the point of view of an untrustworthy narrator, and these days I think it's just going to make them angrier.

So things change. Good. But if it weren't for this nasty pop anomaly I wouldn't have been exposed to "In Germany Before the War" at the perfect time in my life to scare me out of my wits, and at the same time light my imagination on fire by exposing me to the wild mood-shaping power of chord voicing and orchestral arranging. This song represents the first glimmer my young mind ever perceived of the true scope of what just the music part of a song can do—how truly infinite the realm of possibilities is tonally. I still know of no better song to illustrate how clearly the text of a song can be illuminated by its musical habitat. We are never told explicitly what happens to the "little girl" who "lost her way." The music alone conveys that horror. Leaves no doubt. Is this song for everybody? No. It's not a song I would throw on at a BBQ. But it is special to me. Which is the point of this book. Sharing how songs big and small, funny and dark, consoling AND upsetting, all end up rattling around in the same head is, to me, fascinating beyond compare and worthy of some book-length introspection.

I'm also amazed at how funny it is, at least in my opinion, that this song exists in the same universe as "Short People," much less on the same album. A hit single, mind you, the seven-inch of which came in a sleeve that admonished purchasers to keep it stored on a high shelf out of reach of . . . um, you get it. Can you imagine?! So there's that. But "In Germany Before the War" really is a masterpiece of musical storytelling. And I do think about it often when I'm trying to get a recording I'm working on to tell the listener where to look when the words alone can't. When I'm trying my best to get people to look at the river but think of the sea, as the chorus of this song says. A simple couplet that somehow perfectly captures the dissociation of a serial killer and at the same time tells you exactly how music works. How an illusion can be built upon the genuine discomfort of a major melody over a minor chord.

Randy Newman tells us what to look at by showing us what isn't there. With music. I'm still striving to learn how to conjure that type of magic. I want to make things that make people feel and know things without any thinking on their part. It's kind of the whole point. It's why it's so unimportant to dwell upon what songs "mean." If you could just tell someone a melody, music wouldn't be necessary. I might not have understood it at the time I first heard this song, but this is the song I still turn to the most to relearn this beautiful truth about what it is that I aspire to do.

THE UN-COPIED COPY

DUPLICATING UNCLE TUPELO'S FIRST DEMO TAPE ONE
at a time on a dual cassette deck from Sears.

Cutting out and folding the hand-drawn xeroxed
cardboard "J-cards" and inserting them into the ridiculously fragile and unnervingly sharp plastic cassette
cases.

Remembering the specific kind of cuticle damage
loading cassette cases would inevitably cause.

All of these steps feeling like a leap forward into the
modern world of efficiency and automation compared to
our previous process.

Which in the past was, when a bar owner or club
booker would ask, "Do you have a demo tape?" we would
tense up and nod. Then we would solemnly trudge back
to whoever's basement we were practicing in at the time.
Press record on a cheap boom box and record ourselves
playing the four or five songs we considered our "best" . . .

say, "Psycho" by the Sonics, "Hang on Sloopy" (the Remains version), "Are You Gonna Be There (At the Love-In)" by the Chocolate Watchband, and, um . . . "Louie Louie" probably. Press eject, write the name of the band and our phone numbers on the commercially provided track card, and then drive the one and only copy directly back to the bar or club we were hoping would give us a gig. For every bar or club, that's what we did—we'd hand over the only copy. The un-copied copy. For years. It never occurred to us that we could duplicate a cassette until one of us asked why some boom boxes have places for two tapes.

Part of being the bass player in those days meant you were the one responsible for a lot of legwork. Scrounging up gigs, going to Kinko's, flyer-ing telephone poles, etc.

Name the three pieces of gear every bass player needs.

A bass, an amp . . . and a staple gun.

That's how the joke used to go.

DANCING QUEEN

IT'S IMPORTANT IN LIFE TO ADMIT WHEN YOU WERE wrong about something. And although I bristle at the notion that there could ever be such a thing as a "wrong" musical opinion, I was relieved when I finally was able to admit I was colossally wrong about this song (and ABBA in general). I'm happy I can admit it. Maybe even a touch proud of myself for not digging my heels in and hating this song for even a second longer than I had to, unlike some friends I know who are still holding out. To me the weird part is ever feeling like I had to hate something so clearly irresistible.

At the time this song came out there were very strict lines in the sand being drawn between cultural camps. This tune was located deep in "enemy" territory, at the intersection of pop and disco. I personally liked pop radio because occasionally a gem would slip through the cracks. You'd get a "Saturday Night" by the Bay City

Rollers or "You're My Best Friend" by Queen. Or something absurd like "Convoy" would make it on the Top 40 and brighten your day. I was just self-possessed enough as a nine-year-old in 1976 to be able to see how overblown my brother's lectures on the dangers of "bubblegum" music were. So I could tune him out when he'd go on about how my "brain was still developing" and I "must be vigilant against IQ-lowering aspects of TV and pop culture."

But disco was despised by practically everyone I knew (with the exception of the kids who liked to roller skate; that seemed to be where the line was drawn). Basically, meaning that to all of the males older than myself in my extended family sphere, disco had taken on the profile of something legitimately wrong. A world-destroying force that we must all unite against. So it was easy at the time to say, "Okay, I'm not even going to listen to that music because that music SUCKS!" And of course, there was also the additional specter of an added adjective—disco was "gay." And to nine-year-old boys who didn't know any better, *gay* meant "bad." Really bad. And to my teenage cousins wrestling with a bit of sexual ambiguity, *gay* was really scary and really bad. And tragically, even to almost all of the adults I knew, who definitely should have known better, *gay* was bad. Where I grew up, when I grew up, just saying you liked something that had been deemed "gay" meant YOU were gay. It was no joke. Add to this the fact that, musically, disco was a technology-embracing extension of Black American musical forms and, as a movement, seemed to be utterly ignoring the traditional American Black/white racial divide . . . and, well, that's just too much ignorance for even the most confident child (which I was not) to sort through and reject.

I wish I could say that looking back on that time from 2023 makes it hard to believe people were ever so small-minded and bigoted. But of course it's entirely believable because *I'm waving my arms around*.

I'm taking a moment here to make clear to you, the reader, that I do understand the band I'm talking about here was/is white (Swedish! Sooo white!) and straight. It doesn't matter. Or at least it didn't matter at the time, because it was "disco." It was thoroughly demonized, and for all the wrong reasons.

And so through all of the societal forces at play and by my own weakness, I never allowed myself to like it. Until years later, after I'd already started trying to write songs and found myself staring at an overhead speaker in a grocery store aisle (not stoned!) just reeling at this familiar melody and how exuberantly sad it was. "Having the time of your life!" A real come-to-Jesus moment. A real come–to–Agnetha, Björn, Benny, and Anni-Frid moment.

But before that day, I, along with many others, had denied myself undeniable joy. Countless fantastic records and deep grooves were dismissed and derided out of ignorance. Of course, this song and this music was always going to win eventually. Because it's just too special to ignore forever.

There are wrong opinions about music! And to this day, "Dancing Queen" is the song I always think of when I THINK I don't like something. It taught me that I can't ever completely trust my negative reactions. I was burned so badly by this one song being withheld from my heart for so long. I try to never listen to music without first politely asking my mind, and whatever blind spots I'm afflicted with today, to move aside long enough for my gut to be the judge. And even then, if I don't like something I make a mental note to try again in ten years.

Melodies as pure and evocative as the one in "Dancing Queen" don't come along every day. I'm sad for every single moment I missed loving this song. Playing it again right now. Making up for lost spins. I truly recommend spending some time looking for a song you might have unfairly maligned. It feels good to stop hating something. Music is a good place to start if you're interested in forgiveness. For yourself, mostly, I assume. Because records can't really change much over time, but we sure can, and do. Better late than never.

THE MESSAGE

WHAT GENRE OF MUSIC'S BIRTH DO YOU THINK I FEEL the most connected to? Wrong. It's not alt-country. Guess again . . . wrong!

Okay, I'll give you a hint. It's hip-hop. The answer is hip-hop. And that's because I was at the right age during the right moment in history to witness the mind-blowing birth of a new genre. No, I wasn't there at the block parties in the Bronx when turntables transformed into expressive instruments and, along with samplers and drum machines, razed the playing field so level anyone with something to say could now, in fact, get that shit off of their chest.

However, I was there shortly after. Along with practically everyone else alive at the time not living under a rock, I got to be among the first humans to buy a "rap" record. Sugarhill Gang's "Rapper's Delight." And again, it wasn't like I was some twelve-year-old musical adventurer out there alone, blazing a trail with less worldly listeners lagging behind. No. This song was instantly everywhere. Kids I knew who never seemed to show interest in music of any kind were walking around singing "Rock it out baby bubba to the boogity bang bang the boogie to the boogie the beat."

It was exciting beyond belief. The racial divides that generally ruled Top 40 radio (an issue that sadly persists to this day) seemed to disappear for a brief and glorious stretch of time in the late seventies and, to a lesser degree, into the early eighties. Next it was Kurtis Blow's "The Breaks" for me. Which is not as talked about these days. I would imagine I knew the track was due to Kurtis being from the St. Louis area, rather than any indication of or argument for the legitimacy of my status as an "OG." Blondie's "Rapture" technically had some "rapping" on it. Pretty bad "rapping" that, by today's standards, kind of sounds like my margarita-buzzed sister "spitting rhymes" at brunch—"a man from mars / eating cars / going to bars / what the heck / I'll pick up the check"— but I'll accept it. Very cool of them to give it a go.

But the moment that really hammered home the fact that this music was not just some pop music anomaly— a gimmick that would fizzle out once it fell out of fashion, like the wah-wah pedal or yodeling—was when "The Message" by Grandmaster Flash and the Furious Five hit the airwaves and kicked everyone's ass into gear. This was the moment where it became clear that hip-hop was a vitally important whole new form of musical expression. Even a dumb kid like myself could hear it when this song came on the radio. Dylan never wrote anything nearly as incisive and direct. "The answer, my friend, is blowin' in the wind" sounds pretty much like a greeting card next to

> People pissing on the stairs you know they just don't
> care . . .
> Don't push me 'cause I'm close to the edge
> I'm trying not to lose my head

"The Message" is a carved-in-stone moment for me. Every verse is instantly accessible in my memory. I've come to think of this as a type of high-art journalism. Like Woody Guthrie. This is front-lines war correspondence the way the ancients did it. Setting the scene of what it was like to survive the inner-city deprivations of the late seventies and early eighties to a sturdy hypnotic poem, and then sending it out across oceans of time and space with the understanding that being a witness to suffering demands documentation. Haters gonna hate. But witnesses gonna witness. And art gets the last word.

OVERDUBS

LATE AT NIGHT, HELPING SOME FRIENDS (ALSO IN their teens) record their band at a studio in downtown Belleville. Going slow.

Scary-looking biker dude busts in the front door furiously looking for Dave, the guy who owns the studio and is "producing" the session.

Finds Dave under the mixing desk. Drags Dave into the tracking room by his mullet and gives him a merciless beating as we all steer clear in stunned silence. At one point, I swear he played my friend's drums with Dave's head.

Tired and apparently satisfied with the punishment he's delivered, the low-rent Terminator leaves.

Dave, acting as if this is part of his daily routine, pops up off the floor. Bleeding from his mouth and with one eye swollen shut, he asks cheerfully, "Where were we? Overdubs?"

BALANCING ACT

WHEN YOU'RE AN ANGSTY KID, YOU'RE AN EASY mark for angsty songs. It's hard to avoid the very specific, painfully earnest spectacle of asking a parent or love interest or pet to sit down and listen to a record that somehow expresses "exactly" how you feel.

Speaking for myself, these embarrassing scenes from my teenage years most typically were played out at our yellow Formica kitchen table with my mom squinting at me through cigarette smoke, speakers aimed down the stairs from my attic bedroom, my gaze averted, mouthing the words, occasionally lifting my eyes toward my mother's patient and neutral face, trying to gauge whether or not she was "getting it."

For the life of me, I can't figure out why describing this tableau still fills me with something approaching shame. Maybe I'm still worried that letting on about the degree to which I was emotionally dependent upon my mother makes me "less than." Or I suppose it's possible that I'm still feeling a vestigial sense of guilt about the level of indulgence and support I enjoyed at home, when even at the time I was aware of how rare that truly is. Like the urge to conceal an extravagant gift around friends having a tougher time scraping by.

But in reality, I think that what once looked self-flatteringly poignant and unique has been revealed by time to be pretty par for the course. The course being adolescence, naturally. So while the attempt to be better understood by asking someone to look at us through the lens of someone else's song fits the outlines we're all busy trying to color in at "that" age, I will say I'm not sure the songs I was picking as surrogates got much airplay outside of our kitchen. Whenever I think of this song by the Volcano Suns, it feels frozen forever in the amber of my youth. Suspended in the air surrounding my mother's mind striving to understand her sad son's alienation. Head cocked sincerely, leaning into the words. Nodding and tearing up at the tears falling from my cheeks.

How should I act in a crowd?
Should I voice my feelings
For acquaintances?
Should I feel lucky to be a part of the wheeling and
  dealing no matter what is said?
. . . It matters, it matters, it MATTERS TO ME!

I'm glad this song was there for me. It still means a lot to me. It's hard when you feel so many things so deeply. It's even harder when you care a lot and the world keeps not giving a shit.

It still matters to me, and I couldn't have said it better myself.

FRANKIE TEARDROP

IN 1982 BRUCE SPRINGSTEEN PUT OUT A STARK HOME-recorded acoustic album called *Nebraska*. The bulk of the songs put the singer's voice squarely behind the wheel of a car, narrating tales of desperation and redemption. From both sides of the law. It's a desolate record. Beautifully rendered, unmistakably American landscapes place it alongside the short stories of Flannery O'Connor, Capote's *In Cold Blood*, and our sick romanticizing of Charles Starkweather's real-life murder spree. These are all influences directly cited at the time by the Boss himself. And to Bruce's credit, he also made a point of professing his admiration of and his indebtedness to a band little known to most of his audience: Suicide.

I'll be honest, I felt pretty proud of myself for noticing the connection before I heard Mr. Springsteen fess up to the inspiration. Suicide was a band on my radar through sheer luck and good fortune, thanks to the previously discussed odd programming choices of *The Midnight Special*'s "New Wave" episode. But it wasn't like it required a truly sophisticated ear to hear that the vocal tics and lyrical phrasing on *Nebraska* were directly lifted from Suicide's singer, Alan Vega. It was obvious, but only if you'd ever heard Suicide. Which made me cool because, again, not a lot of people had at the time. Plus, I was probably in the running to be considered among the youngest of all the people on the planet (or at least in my hometown) who could claim awareness of said protopunk band, Suicide. First band to call themselves punk, by the way—in 1970, no less!

Now, with all due respect to Bruce, there's a big difference between the real deal and a loving homage. And while Bruce's portrayal of the desolation of the American psyche is nuanced and convincing in an actorly way, when you hear something like the Suicide song "Frankie Teardrop," it makes Bruce sound like John Denver. It still stands at the limit of the amount of torment and terror that can be captured on a recording. *Nebraska*'s characters sound like they come from a modern western— beautifully lit, acted out on blacktop in bucket seats. Serious and moralistic. Good art. What Alan Vega is doing, on the other hand, is hard to fathom. No one in their right mind would want to go where he's determined to take us. It sounds like he doesn't have a choice. And if he has to listen to the sound of a murdered murderer's tortured screams from the depths of hell breaking apart his brain, it's only fair he gets to claw at us from the grave.

Seriously, though. Don't listen to this track if you aren't in the mood to be legitimately upset. Also, pro parenting tip—don't cue this song up on a dark country road for your young teenage child driving them home from an aborted sleepover gone bad. I know someone who did that (me) and nearly a decade later it still comes up when my parental judgment is in question.

SEVENTIES
CAPRICE CLASSIC

ONE A.M., MAKING THE DECISION TO ABANDON MY seventies Caprice Classic after nearly an hour of struggling, pushing, gunning, turning tires, spinning tires, rocking, don't forget to rock it . . . trying to get myself unstuck from the fucking ice and snow—excuse me, "wintry mix"—in an alley behind a friend's apartment in the Soulard Market area of St. Louis.

Figuring I should remove the license plates to avoid being fined for illegal dumping or whatnot.

Desperately fumbling at the rusty screws with my bare, frozen fingers. Giving up. Then, Hulk-like, furiously folding and unfolding and yanking at the virtually indestructible aluminum alloy the state of Illinois made license plates out of. Finally tearing off the weakened tags. Triumph!

Burying the mangled shards of my Illinois license

plates in the snow. Behind some trash cans. Just to be safe.

Have I mentioned this happened before I quit drinking?

No? Okay. Well, I'm pretty sure I had been drinking on this particular evening.

So, I guess the plan was . . .

Um . . . I'm not sure if I understand what "the plan" was, even now.

I suppose I was tired and drunk and I had no way to call a tow truck. And/or I was too dumb to think of a more responsible plan. Even the thought of asking a friend to help seems to have slipped my mind. I guess because it would have involved walking a few blocks each way in the bitter cold.

Actually, it just came to me. The plan was, I wanted to go to sleep. Like, right away. If the car was there in the morning, then I'd have a clearer head (as if) to deal with it. Or . . . maybe all of the snow and ice would melt?

And if it wasn't there?

Spoiler alert: It was not. I assume it was towed by the city of St. Louis to some impound lot. I never followed up because I was afraid I'd get slapped with a fine. And in those days there was a very real chance a municipal fine might actually exceed the three hundred or so dollars I had invested in this bald-tired bucket of rusting American steel.

So I had no car. I didn't deserve to have a car.

And I think that's the judgment I made at the moment I committed to ditching the car.

I think about this episode of my life most often when I'm watching some true-crime documentary. Where after hours and hours of interrogation a couple of belligerent cops get some scared kid to falsely confess to murdering his whole family.

Most of the time the problem is that they're all just tired and want to go home. I have empathy for all parties. The cops don't have a clue and have wasted too much time already talking to an innocent kid to even begin to stomach the idea of having to start all over with some new lead.

And the kid? Well, there but for the grace of you-know-who go I.

Because I learned a couple of things about myself in that alley that night.

1. I would absolutely admit to murdering anyone and anything if the promise of getting to go home and go to sleep were being dangled as the carrot.

2. I would absolutely murder and bury a license plate if a hopelessly ice-mired car stood between me and a bed.

I'M NOT IN LOVE

ONE OF THE AMAZING THINGS SONGS CAN DO IN the mind of a single listener is transform, over time, from something reviled and loathed to the point of avoidance—an instant radio-dial-lunge type of track—to something breathtakingly beautiful and essential.

Take this song, by 10cc, for example. When this song came out, I hated it so much I actually kind of feared it. There was something about the middle section that made me feel "super icky," as I would have put it at the time. The part where it sounds like you're coming out of a coma, stuck inside your body, unable to move or communicate but aware of the people whispering around your hospital bed—that part really bothered me, and describing it now, I must admit, has reawakened some vestigial anxiety I was in the process of claiming to have transcended.

But that doesn't change the fact that this song, over time, went from Brussels sprouts to cake in my ears' taste buds, somehow. Or I guess, more accurately, it went from my eight-year-old opinion of Brussels sprouts to my current grown-ass status as a person who can't get enough of those odd roll-y little balls of plant stuff.

So yeah, I'm basically just saying our tastes change. What we want from a song can evolve. And again, the song itself obviously doesn't change. We do. We notice and appreciate things we missed. In the case of this track, it's not surprising that a kid, unschooled and un-interested in the ways of love, might miss the pitch-black dark humor of the lyric

I keep your picture upon the wall
It hides a nasty stain that's lying there
So don't you ask me to give it back
I know you know it doesn't mean that much to me

That line alone might have warranted a reevaluation. But the thing that kills me now when I hear this song is how masterfully conceived it is. From the arrangement to the tonal textures chosen, this recording creates its own internal logic. A feat of engineering few songs ever come close to. It sounds like no other song on earth, an alien-sounding song about alienation, and at the same time it was so successful at drawing people in that it became a massive hit. Otherwise, I wouldn't have heard it as a kid and then kept bumping into it on the radio the rest of my life until it wound up in this book. Where I'm telling you how great it is.

CONNECTION

I HAVE A TON OF FAVORITE RECORDS. A LOT OF THEM are records that had already withstood the test of time well before they ever landed on my turntable. Your Beatles, your Dylans, your Supremes, your Ronettes . . . you know, your basic wide-swath pop-rock-centric canon. Maybe an equal number to that are records that I got to buy firsthand (punk era onward through the indie years to today) or albums I discovered as reissues of lesser-known artists—records that people would pretend they already knew but were really new to most of us. Records that deserved an audience and finally found one among my generation of record freaks (things like Os Mutantes and Karen Dalton come to mind).

And then there are a handful of records that feel like I'm the only one in the world who cares about them. Records that make you feel the urge to evangelize. I know that it's unlikely there could truly be any publicly released music that found its way to my heart alone. But some records really get overlooked, and it's strange when you realize a record that's become a constant companion reliably draws blank stares when brought up. Even with your biggest music-snob pals.

Now, occasionally you really do fall in love with something that comes by its obscurity the old-fashioned way—by being extremely rare in terms of the number manufactured and its nearly nonexistent commercial appeal. Those are the records that get buffed like badges at the counters of indie record stores—"What?! You've never heard Plaid Turd? Oh man. Their first EP is easily in my top five all-time crap-core slabs." I do believe there's a certain amount of pity warranted toward a person who would state something like that.

But it should also be noted that, no. No it isn't. The person saying this is not telling the truth. Plaid Turd, good as they may be (I just made them up), are not favorite-record material. That poor nerd has built an identity around records. More specifically, they're the kind of person who has little to no self-esteem outside of the extremely niche body of knowledge some maladaptive obsession has bestowed upon them. People who act like the farther an artist is away from having an actual audience is a reliable measure of musical worth. You know who I'm talking about. And you know who you are. I see myself in you. My judgment is harsh but fair. Self-examination has revealed these truths.

But that's not what I'm here to talk about. I'm more fascinated by the lesser-known or even deeply maligned works of artists that are otherwise highly considered. And how I think it's cool that a record like *Between the Buttons* by the Rolling Stones can achieve a cherished status based on a few unlikely twists of fate. Like how in my house growing up, a very high percentage of the records we owned were purchased from bargain bins. Cutouts—records marked for clearance by having a triangular piece of the album jacket's upper right-hand corner cut out or similarly defaced. If it weren't for cutouts, I doubt my older siblings would have ever been allowed to buy a Stones record. By the time I came around, they had all mostly left home, but their records remained. So my favorite Stones record is the one no one gave a shit about when I was growing up. I know that now it's regarded as a classic, but I still rarely see it mentioned alongside the more commonly accepted Stones canon. Mick Jagger himself has described *Between the Buttons* as "more or less rubbish."

Well, I think Mr. Jagger's opinion is rubbish. Because this shit slaps. (Am I saying that right?)

Listen to "Connection." I've been trying to write my version of "Connection" for about forty years. It's in my DNA. My favorite song on my favorite Stones album. All because a record company miscalculated and overshot an already ridiculously high demand just enough for it to end up discounted and thus fit my folks' meager budget.

TRAUMATIZING TOILET

FOR YEARS I THOUGHT THAT MY MIND HAD SIMPLY enhanced or possibly even fabricated the utterly traumatizing toilet at CBGB's. Could it have possibly been in the open on a riser in the corner of the room? With no WALLS?!

Yes. Yes, that's exactly how it was. An installation at the Met and photos confirm it. And yes—I was scarred for life by the absolute necessity to employ this facility.

FOREVER PARADISE

IN THE LATE SEVENTIES THE UNDERTONES WERE thought of as the Irish Ramones. Checks out. Their members came from places with names like Bogside and Creggan. They formed in Derry. And if you've ever listened to their first record, you know the Ramones inspiration is an undeniable shoe that fits. They were a great band. Bright, tuneful three-chord punk rock. Catchy melodies. Nowhere near as lyrically demented as their New York counterparts, but still in the general ballpark of the Ramones.

A lot of classic angsty pop subject matter. Boy/girl troubles. Girl/boy/other boy troubles. Not much about "the Troubles" troubles, but who can blame them for craving a little escape. It was energetic kid stuff. Wildly effective, simple broken-heart cures in the form of two-minute-thirty-second blasts of bummed-out joy. They had the hooks for hits, too. In the UK they got on the charts with their first single, "Teenage Kicks." It didn't go to number one, but before he died the legendary BBC DJ John Peel did claim it was his all-time favorite song. They did crack the top ten in the UK with a single off of their second record, the utterly charming "My Perfect Cousin."

In the States nothing ever really got going for them. I knew about them because I used to read the imported British rock tabloids (*NME*, *Melody Maker*, *Sounds*) cover to cover at my local record store. Occasionally, I'd buy an issue just to re-up the record clerks' tolerance of my loitering. The music press in the UK was incredibly fickle. They fully embraced the role of tabloid journalism. The pressure to sell a new issue every week— find new bands, create new sensations, generate fashion crazes—made them insane. They made it sound like the British bands were reinventing the concept of music hourly.

At some point I figured out the fever pitch of excitement surrounding every new band they championed was a bit of a scam. I think it was reading a headline calling the band Haircut 100 "exciting" with a cover photo of six guys with cable-knit sweaters tied over their shoulders, James Spader–style, that finally allowed the penny to drop on what was really going on with these mags.

But once again, I have to acknowledge the good with the bad. Because the Undertones went on to make one of my favorite albums of all time. These sleazy rags with their questionable motives hipped me to the Undertones. And by the time they were no longer the hot new band gracing their covers, I happened to still care about them enough to buy their third album, *Positive Touch*. I also liked their second album, *Hypnotised*. Similar to their first lyrically, but musically searching and hinting at a sophistication far beyond the three-chord structures of their debut. But nothing could have prepared me for the quantum leap that *Positive Touch* represented when it came out in 1981.

Positive Touch has been my constant companion since then, even though it quickly disappeared from even the UK charts, never mind never making the US charts. I can think of no other pop record quite like it. I'm always inspired by the inventiveness of its arrangements. Bands are human-scale miracles. Any band that sounds good playing together has created magic. But when a band throws away a formula as sturdy and true as the one the Undertones were so good at, and believes in themselves and each other enough to find a way to sound like only themselves—to create a music that exists only because they looked for it somewhere inside of themselves—knowing that there's a record they want to hear and that the only way they'll ever get to hear it is to make it themselves . . . Well, that's a miracle made of miracles.

"Forever Paradise" is the last song on side two. The

preferred last song of the evening on school nights. It's a bit eerie. Piano notes sleepwalking into the mist. Beautiful androgynous vocal. Fractures into an extended backward sound collage that puts itself together again for the last chorus:

Forever and ever
Forever and ever
Forever and ever
Forever and ever
Paradise

My dreams often play this song in the background.

At a time in my life when everything felt like forever but not much resembled paradise, this song was a comfort. And falling asleep to it was as perfectly content as I ever got in those days.

SATAN, YOUR KINGDOM MUST COME DOWN

HAVE YOU EVER HEARD OF A MAN NAMED JOHN CO-hen? Whether you have or haven't, it's probably safe to say you're unaware of the outsize role he played in shaping the impression Uncle Tupelo made on the world. He, along with Harry Smith and his *Anthology of American Folk Music*, was among the very first to open a window into our country's musical past and say, "Hey, get a load of how wild this stuff is!" The band he formed with some fellow travelers in the late fifties to document and perform old-time folk tunes, the New Lost City Ramblers, and the albums they recorded, is where Jay Farrar and I first heard the Carter Family song "No Depression." In fact, it was only much later, after naming our debut album *No Depression* and performing the song for years, that we finally got to hear the Carters' original recording, the one that the New Lost City Ramblers had learned the song from.

So right there a big chunk of what Uncle Tupelo is known for wouldn't have happened without our hero John Cohen. If you have the time, you really should look him up and marvel at his accomplishments. But the thing he did that most changed my life was travel around the rural South and collect songs. He wasn't the only person doing this, of course. I cherish his work alongside that of John and Alan Lomax and many other folklorists and musicologists. Their belief in the world-shaping power of song has, no doubt, led me here to this book. Admittedly, my work here is much more internal and less academic in its conception, but I do believe I'm guided by a similar passion to share not just songs but their ability to get up and walk around and form new landscapes as they travel.

To be specific about John Cohen's contribution to our recorded history, I'd like to point you in the direction of *High Atmosphere: Ballads and Banjo Tunes from Virginia and North Carolina*, a collection of field recordings done by John circa 1965 and subsequently released in 1975 on Rounder Records.

Just a side note on how hard it was to get your hands on archival folk recordings like these by the time the mideighties rolled around. "Out of print" usually meant "good luck ever even seeing a copy." Your best shot at owning a title like *High Atmosphere* was to check it out from a local library and never return it. Which is something I would never do (but I knew a guy who would).

My copy of *High Atmosphere* was legit, though. I found it in the used bins. It was a fluke. The type of lucky find that for Jay Farrar and me would lead to deep resentment in the heart of the party fortune had frowned upon. Resulting in whispered arguments, side by side, no eye contact, still dutifully flipping through the racks—"No! I'm not letting you buy it! I'll let you tape it! It's not my fault you started in the M's."

Uncle Tupelo recorded three songs we had learned off of this same album, including the one we're about to discuss—"Satan, Your Kingdom Must Come Down." It's a very old-sounding song sung by a very old-sounding man named Frank Proffitt. The premise is, you got it, Satan's kingdom must, you know, come down.

How we go about making that happen changes as the song progresses. First, we're going to pray. If that doesn't work (spoiler: it won't), we'll sing. Still no luck? Then we're going to have to shout. "Shout until they tear your kingdom down." So the question is, why would this nonbeliever (me, not Frank. Frank is a believer without a doubt) find this song so utterly compelling and cathartic? So much so that I wanted to sing it myself. Why did I believe I could sing this song convincingly? I think it was something about how old it all felt. How clearly it made the struggle to deal with all the bullshit an eternal ordeal. This song and performance helped me form a connection to the angst of the past. It's silly sounding, perhaps, but, god, did it feel good to know that the crappy way I felt wasn't new. Granted, this isn't what most people would ever get out of this song. Surely I was projecting at IMAX proportions. But I still feel it. And I stand by my interpretation's validity.

Because what I was really searching for in those days was authenticity. I craved it. There was a deep need to feel like I wasn't always being lied to. That there were, in fact, "real" things in the world. Not everything was an agreed-upon fiction like the flag, or dollar bills, or sports "teams."

Or, of course, the shared delusions of religion. Punk rock records gave me a lot of hope, but they weren't fool-proof. Bands could burn you by "selling out." Which is kind of a quaint concept these days. It was dumb. But it really did hurt at the time.

So recordings like this—where one isn't even sure the person singing understands that they're being re-corded, and, let's face it, by now they're almost certainly dead—became the gold standard for authenticity in our world. This music was unassailably pure. The fact that this song refers to Satan, one of the top three hallucina-tions of all time, made not one bit of difference. What I heard then, and what I still hear today, is what I always thought was written in the margins of punk music. The defiant dream that for good to triumph over every fucking thing in the world that sucks, all of the evil, all of the greed, all of the phoniness, all of it, everything you hate—all you have to do is keep singing.

Don't stop. Shout if you have to. Whatever you think "Satan's kingdom" might be, however strong a hold you might think the "devils" have on the world, it's no match for a teenager in their bedroom listening to a broken voice and a rattling banjo echoing some truth through the trees.

BROWN RECLUSE
SPIDER BITE

REMEMBERING THE TOUR BUS DRIVER WHO SHOWED up in Chicago along with his wife. Our road manager at the time said, "We only hired you." Bus driver, pulling back his coat, revealing a gun at his hip. He said, "She's comin' along. 'Cause I gotta brown recluse spider bite on my leg, and she's gonna help keep it clean."

Waking up at the hotel one morning and realizing the bus, and all of our gear, was gone. Asking where they'd been when they returned two days later, only to hear that they'd been "visitin' friends."

Surprised to find out, in the middle of the night, that the wife was driving, and the husband was sleeping. Our road manager asked them to pull over and switch drivers, and she said, "That's fine, I was done with my shift anyway." She pulled into a truck stop and bought some hard lemonade. At this point, our nerves were wrecked, so a lot of us were in the front lounge, not sleeping, listening through the curtain to what they were doing. He was driving now, and she was drinking. I heard her say, "You want one?" and he said, "I'll have a swaller." And she poured it into his coffee mug.

Back in those days, we couldn't do anything about much, because we'd get stranded. We weren't high on the list with the bus companies.

GOD DAMN JOB

UP UNTIL NOW I'VE BEEN WRITING ABOUT RECORDED
music, primarily. Aside from thinking my cousin wrote
"Takin' Care of Business," all of the previous chapters
have been about songs that exist as records. You can
cross-reference them—maybe hear them for the first
time, or see if they hit your ears any different after reading about them. It's safe to assume most of these songs
are accessible through the wonders of modern technology, and accessible without a whole lot of trouble. If
I tell you I had some type of life-shaping spiritual event
listening to, let's say, ELO's "Telephone Line," you can
go hear for yourself and test whether or not that magic
works on you as well.

This song, however, is different. Even though there is
a record to reference, a record that I own, purchased the
following day after the event I'm about to describe, this
song is one I first heard live, and it was delivered to me

like a punch to the chest. Viscerally. I can still feel it. It was a once-in-a-lifetime moment. Something I witnessed with my own eyes and ears, even though now it only exists inside me as a memory. A crazy, cherished memory. The kind of memory that ends up sounding both overblown and pale when stated out loud, like pointing at a ghost no one else can see.

But to me, this moment was so . . . um, momentous, that it feels like it could take the rest of this book to put it into the proper perspective. Or maybe it's more like trying to convince you that I once saw lightning strike a duck or that I was walking around a hotel lobby hungry one time and a vending machine I glanced at longingly spontaneously began spitting out snacks at my feet. Just one of those slices of life that, when recounted, gets one's mundane mixed up in one's fantasy and one's fantasy mixed up in one's mundane. A precarious tale to tell—I picture you nodding off, the way I drift away when someone tries to tell me about the dream they had last night. "Wow, that's crazy," I interject as I give up on trying to form a corollary mental picture. Point is, it's nearly impossible to get these moments pinned down in writing with any shape resembling a true epiphany. Because the part that's missing—the part that can't ever be completely conveyed—is you (or me in this instance . . . er, you know what I mean). And how the stage these pivotal scenes are acted out on is set against a vast internal backdrop no one else has enough mental energy (or mind paint, to further the metaphor) to complete.

So I'm going to ask you to help me out a little. Please. If you don't mind. Try to picture a moment from your youth when you felt empty—weary beyond your years, bored with everything, including yourself. Maybe even more than a little bit sad for no real reason. Did you ever feel like that? I have not met many people who can't relate, but if you're one of them, I'm happy for you. I also think you're a liar or a sociopath.

Got it? Are you there, swinging slowly back and forth in that dull malaise? Okay, there you are.

Yes. Now picture a band you've basically never heard of, a band that also happens to be the best rock band of all time, walking out onto a poorly lit stage to a smattering of golf claps and a few ambiguous *woo*s.

You've been waiting for the show to begin with a few friends and a couple of other kids in the humiliatingly named Kiddie Corral section of the club. You're excited to see X, another great band and the reason you're here. The Replacements are a band you've kind of heard of, but you can't remember ever being very impressed with supporting acts. Maybe you're a little bit relieved that the opening act isn't Fools Face again. The parachute-panted and rattailed "New Wave" band that seemed to have some deal with the club that gave them first dibs on being added to the bill any time a band that could even remotely be described as punk/New Wave would roll through St. Louis. All I really remember about them is that they had a lot of belts—red belts, white belts, and black belts, none of which appeared to be functioning with any beltlike usefulness. Oh, and they had synthesizers on those hideous A-frame racks (a half measure for guys who wanted to look cool standing up playing a keyboard but weren't ready to fully commit to the keytar), which was a real deal-breaker for me and most of my friends at the time. They'd play and dance their hearts out in front of an audience that had paid to see someone like Hüsker Dü, just to get booed and have whole cups of beer thrown at them. I didn't like them, but it always made me a bit sad and I could never really figure out why they wanted those slots. So I thought maybe they'd reached the limit of the abuse they were willing to subject themselves to and had finally decided to sit this show out.

So out come the Replacements, looking like they're all wearing some combination of clothes from a specialty shop for tall toddlers and hand-me-downs from the Clash. Fucked-up hair, spray-painted guitars, effortlessly cool in a way I'd never seen before. Fashion without even a hint of trying . . .

"I NEED A GODDAMN JOB, I NEED A GODDAMN JOB, I REALLY NEED A GODDAMN JOB, I NEED A GODDAMN JOB!"

And then the chorus . . .

"GODDAMNIT, GODDAMNIT, GODDAMN! I NEED A GODDAMN JOB!"

By now Paul Westerberg had already leaned so far into his microphone that he'd fallen face-first off of the front of the stage onto the empty dance floor. Where he remained for the rest of the song, singing and playing guitar uninterrupted, in various positions: Prone, balancing on his forehead with his mouth pressed against the mic. On his back, craning his neck sideways, 100 percent commitment to the bit.

Except it wasn't a bit. It was as real as anything I'd ever seen. The self-liberating promise of rock 'n' roll, punk rock, whatever you want to call it, come to life, directly in front of my very eyes! I knew I hadn't really witnessed the birth of rock 'n' roll. But I also knew it didn't matter. Because it had been invented inside me that day. This was as close as I'd ever get. I knew what it was. I'd read about it. I'd heard it and believed in it. Like I'm sure people must have read about the lightbulb and marveled at the thought before they ever got to stand in a once-dark room illuminated by electricity. My world shone bright in front of me. I embraced it. I didn't understand it. And I still don't. But it lighted my way.

It wasn't "I need a job and I can't find one." It was "The only thing worse than needing a job is having one." Everything that we're all expected to do and trust and believe in is a total fucking drag. It said to me this above all else: Job or not, I am free—school or not, I am free—as long as this exists—this feeling—this moment where nothing else in the world matters—I will survive—this is where I will choose to live. This is where you will find me.

RAMBLIN' MAN

GATHER 'ROUND, KIDS, AND LET ME TELL YOU THE story of White Pride. Like everywhere else in the 1980s, the St. Louis metropolitan area had a hardcore punk rock scene. Not a big one, but big enough for the punk rock zine *Maximum Rocknroll* to check in every now and then.

White Pride, one of the more notorious bands around town, was a tight little outfit made up of a Jew (lead vox), a half-Chinese guy (who played guitar in full Nazi uniform), another guy who appeared to be of some vague and decidedly non-Aryan ancestry (bass), and a terrifying juvenile delinquent who played a snakeskin drum kit and could spit farther than anyone I've ever seen— continuously launching loogies from behind his kit, back and forth like a lawn sprinkler, over his bandmates' heads and into the pit, for the entire show. Given their mixed pedigree and the fact that Jim, their lead vocalist, looked like a filthy hippie (picture Jim from *Taxi* but with the disposition of a taller, angrier Manson and you're close), their whole shtick came across as pretty solid satire. In reality, the band was made up of mostly older musicians, guys who could really play, who couldn't resist poking some fun at the knuckleheads sporting swastikas and whatnot.

So they named themselves White Pride, threw together some hardcore punk rock songs with unspeakable lyrics, and booked some gigs opening for big-deal national punk bands like Circle Jerks. It was a perfect plan except for one teensy tiny flaw. They were so terrifyingly good at punk rock, and the audiences they played for were so terrifyingly dumb, most people didn't get the joke. I got it. I got that it was a joke. But that didn't make it a good joke or less scary. Still, it's hard to fault them for not stating it explicitly, and I understand that to them clarification would have taken the sting out of the satire. Plus, I'm sure they were thinking the Chinese guy would do the trick and they would never have to explain themselves.

Eventually, they did pull the plug on the whole thing, but not before it all got seriously out of hand. To this day their demos and lone seven-inch single go for big bucks among neo-Nazi collector creeps. Years later, after they shut the band down, I got to be friends with most of them. A couple of the guys got into buying and selling vintage guitars. Bob (the partially Chinese rockabilly Nazi, as we called him, with an interest in expediency and accuracy—there were always lots of Bobs) even toured with Uncle Tupelo briefly as our guitar tech. Their drummer went on to form the legendary Drunks with Guns and eventually join local punk juggernaut Ultraman.

And the guy I was most afraid of, Jim, put together a band called Rugburn with his brother and some other kick-ass musician weirdos. They wore matching pastel polyester tuxes and they'd open up their show with the song "Sunshine on My Shoulders" by John Denver. Except they would change the words to "Rugburn on my shoulders makes me happy, Rugburn on my forehead makes me cry," and "Rugburn almost always makes me HI . . . We're Rugburn!"

Jim and a few of the other guys in the band lived in (or squatted in, I honestly don't know, nor does it matter to our little tale here) an abandoned carpet warehouse they referred to as the "Rugbarn." It was a giant wide-open space, every inch of which was covered in carpet. Not like a single, lovely wall-to-wall short pile. They had taken all of the mismatched carpet remnants left behind by the previous owner and installed them piecemeal onto every available surface in the building. Even the ceiling was carpeted. I know all of this because one night, for some forgotten reason (pity, probably), someone in Rugburn invited me and a few friends over to a party they were throwing after one of their shows.

We were stunned. In our eyes, these were our elders. Rugburn and their friends represented the coolest of the cool to us. Men and women wielding unthinkable power over every living thing in our tiny little scene. You know, local luminaries. We were terrified walking in. It was dark. The party was already in full swing. And by "in full swing" I mean that there were people lounging around on giant rolls of industrial flooring drinking beer with some Coltrane playing softly in the distance. But it occurred to us that the calm could still be a ruse. Like I said, it was dark. Maybe our eyes hadn't adjusted yet and something super scary and satanic was happening in some corner of the room yet to come into focus.

We stood still. Unacknowledged. And just as our sense of danger was fading . . . Jim. The tall, scary singer from White Pride. The one I've had nightmares about. That dude. Jim. Stands up in the middle of the room wearing a fucking banjo and launches into an incredible bluegrass version of "Ramblin' Man" by the Allman Brothers. People are hooting and clapping along. Jim's face is full of sincerity and joy. Just delightful.

I learned something very important that night. Up until that point I had accepted the false premise that punk rock, and art in general, required a coherent philosophy to sustain itself. That lines in the sand must be drawn. Gates must be kept. To make revolutionary art (whatever that is) the past must be razed. Slashed and burned and salted. With one deftly strummed banjo adaptation of a southern rock classic I was relieved of that nonsense. Life's too short to postpone that kind of joy. And for what? "Punk" was never the same.

BLUE NOTE

SOMEWHERE IN THE LATE EIGHTIES, BEFORE WE HAD any records out, Uncle Tupelo got a call out of the blue offering us the opening slot for Warren Zevon. At the Blue Note. In Columbia, Missouri.

That night!

Driving the three hours or so from Belleville to the Blue Note to see our favorite bands was common practice in those days. Black Flag, Pixies, Tex and the Horseheads . . . just to name a few.

So, being offered a show on that stage was pretty much the pinnacle of our aspirations at the time.

Saying yes. Or, "Fuck yeah!" rather. Loading up and heading on our way within an hour of the call.

Loading our gear in as Warren Zevon was finishing his sound check.

Being informed that none of Warren Zevon's stage setup would be moved to make space for our gear. Including the grand piano center stage. We were told to figure out how to set up our amps and drums around their equipment.

We were also informed that for our set we would be allowed to use a whopping two channels on the mixing board. Two! So basically we had two vocal mics, and nothing else would be reinforced through the PA.

Looking at the rest of the stage, where Warren Zevon's band was set up. There were microphones literally everywhere. The drum kit had no less than ten. I swear they even had their guitar stands mic'd.

Scanning the stage for any reasonable amount of space for my bass amp. I noticed Timothy B. Schmit from the fucking Eagles making a few last-minute tweaks to his bass sound. Turning knobs on a bass rig that I could hear, clearly, being fed through the front-of-house speakers. A shiny, new, very expensive bass amp in exactly the spot I would have most liked to put my piece-of-shit Peavey bass amp. (The amp I had spray-painted "Pickle River" on for some reason.)

"Hey," I thought, "since only one bass player can play at one time and since Timothy B. Schmit already has a nice sound happening in exactly the place I would love to be able to stand during our set . . . well, maybe he'll be a dear and let me just plug my bass into his rig?"

"Excuse me, Mr. Timothy B. Schmit? Ummm . . . yeah, you guys sound great. Say, I was just wondering, since they're only giving us two mics and we drove all this way, and on account of me not really having anywhere to put my stuff . . . would it be okay with you if I just plugged into your shit? I'd totally put the knobs back the way you have them now. I'm really good about that . . ."

Timothy B. Schmit holding up one finger signaling me to stop talking. Angrily, to his bass tech, "DO NOT LET HIM"—me—"TOUCH FUCKING ANYTHING."

Almost thirty years later, I sat with Mavis Staples in the Obamas' box at the Kennedy Center Honors, next to the Eagles' box. Timothy B. Schmit sat mere feet away from me.

I don't think he recognized me.

I didn't bring it up.

I wanted to.

But it was Mavis's night.

I think I was reminded of this story by the many Zevon cover requests I've received over the years. And maybe as a way to explain why they've all gone unfulfilled. I never really gave him much of a chance after that night. I hated that whole scene. It's obviously my personal issue. I understand the connection many people have to Zevon's records. I would never want to diminish that for anyone.

When I think about this story, I cringe at all the times in my life where my perceived status and behavior toward people needing some grace and acknowledgment from me might have put someone off of my music forever. But the experience at the Blue Note, at that age, was hurtful to me. Of course, now, with hindsight, I understand the ridiculousness and presumptuousness of my request to use the poor guy's precious, personalized bass amplifier. But geez, a simple "Sorry, pal" would've been nice.

HISTORY LESSON-
PART II

"OUR BAND COULD BE YOUR LIFE." I GET EMOTIONAL just typing those words. I might not have formulated that exact sentence in my mind back in 1984, but what it said to me was exactly what I most dreamed someone would say to me when I first heard these words.

This song looms so large in my own personal origin story I almost overlooked writing about it. I've been craning my neck looking up to the heavens picking stars out of the sky—songs that have illuminated my path and elevated my hopes. But this song is the ground on which I stand. There is no other song that comes anywhere close to defining who I was, what I wished to be, and hopefully where I will always work, and never lose sight of.

During interviews I've given as the band I've been in has endured, and grown, over the better part of three decades, I've frequently been asked, "What are your goals?" And the answer I've most often given to this boilerplate journalistic inquiry has been to claim my highest goal is "getting to keep doing what I do." More recently I've been adding the semi-defeated-sounding phrase "I outlived my dreams a long time ago"—not to sound dramatic but because it's true.

"History Lesson—Part II" was that dream put into not just words but a lived and shared practice and example. The Minutemen was what we (Uncle Tupelo) wanted to be. Sonically, we were informed by them; lyrically, we were emboldened by them; but beyond all of the artistic influence, what we most wanted—what we most saw in them—was a genuine strategy for living that felt both accessible and exalted. More than any of their peers, they spoke to us clearly: Start your own band. Get in the van. What are you waiting for? It was an easy ethos to embrace. It was altruistic and human scaled. Be honest! Make some noise with your friends. Spread the word.

So, for me, once we got past the point where we had a record and a van and gigs to play, I had "made it." Everything that has happened beyond that—bigger stages, record sales, Grammys?!—I've looked at as a challenge to live up to but never as something worthy of a belief system to adhere to. Each treacherous step up the proverbial ladder of success has been taken knowing the comforting fact that nothing has ever made me as happy as having a show to play and a way to get to it.

I ask myself all the time, "Would I still want to tour,

make records, write songs, if the whole scope of my currently pretty cushy lifestyle had to be scaled back to the basics?" "Hell yes!" is the enthusiastic response my heart and brain always give me. And I know it's true, because I have a family of friends and acquaintances equally committed to the simple dream laid out in this one song. Some back in the van after years of buses and stardom, even, and others who never left the van.

In fact, Mike Watt himself has never stopped. Not even after losing D., his best friend, in a catastrophic late-night van accident in the desert a year and a half after this song was released. It was a brutal loss. When he died, in the eighties, it seemed impossible. It felt like a rumor none of us could bring ourselves to believe. In part because of how much life, joy, and sincerity we had just heard him sing in "History Lesson—Part II." "Mr. Narrator, this is Bob Dylan to me . . . but I was E. Bloom and Richard Hell, Joe Strummer and John Doe," and then the heart-stopping last line, "Me and Mike Watt, playin' guitar."

Uncle Tupelo used to play this song in rehearsals and I used to sing the last line as "Me and Jay Farrar, playin' guitar," which used to embarrass Jay a little, I think. And even though we didn't keep that band together, I think it's worth sharing that I still hear that lyric as a testament to Jay's and my friendship and commitment to each other at the time. And I don't think it hurts at all to admit that I may never stand on a stage with him again, but some part of me will always just be "playin' guitar" with Jay. And I doubt there'd be much to share here in this book without this song and a friendship that mirrored its wisdom.

By the way, I bought a T-shirt directly from D. Boon after the Minutemen show Jay and I saw at Mississippi Nights in St. Louis shortly before D. died. He was sweaty and kind and I treasure our brief, wordless interaction. The shirt read "The Roar of the Masses Could Be Farts." Yet another example of how far ahead of their time they were.

LITTLE JOHNNY JEWEL

ONE NIGHT AFTER INGESTING A MISMANAGED AMOUNT of pot cookies, I experienced something I've since learned has a name: ego death. Not only was it not a good time, it was a complete pain in the ass for everyone around me. Which happened to be a van full of my Wilco bandmates and crew. I don't know if you know this, but a packed van isn't a great place to have a meltdown. Also not great—being in a van with someone staring into the abyss. So in hindsight, my heart goes out to all involved.

The evening, when it began, had been beautiful. We were on our way to Wilco's first official show at Liberty Lunch in Austin, Texas, for something called South by Southwest (at the time a showcase festival for newer bands that barely resembled its current incarnation). Everyone was in a good mood. Making good time.

Oklahoma zooming by. Vast expanses of flat prairieland rolling out away from the highway left and right. Half a dozen distant lightning storms dotting the horizon. Spectacular.

Then my brain began to glitch. "Hey, guys, maybe we should grab some food?" I floated the idea knowing it rarely gets rejected. The thought I had was that maybe the beautiful, surreal landscape we were weaving through was too overwhelmingly majestic. I needed to get myself back on terra firma. Find my bearings. Decompress a bit in a comfortable, familiar space. Luckily there was a Taco Bell at the next exit.

Again, things started off lovely. Brightly lit. Everyone ordered their tacos and Taco Supremes and burritos and Burrito Supremes. Staff was unusually chipper. Lots of laughing. In fact, I remember thinking to myself, "This is the most fun I've ever had." And I think it might have truly been. Right up until the moment the face of the Taco Bell employee looking at me from behind the register spun around like a roulette wheel and landed on Beelzebub. Everything seemed to change in an instant. But this time it didn't feel like a passing wave of existential dread. This felt like something had truly broken inside of me. It felt permanent. Between this moment and getting back in the van, my memory gets blurry. I see brief images, like I'm watching a TED Talk PowerPoint presentation on the worst moments of my life—"Here you are vomiting and sobbing, and here we see you re-wrapping your burrito for later, since you were psychotic, not stupid."

Once everyone got me calmed down enough to get back in the van, the consensus was to let me pick the music for a while. One of my favorites at the time (and now) was *The Blow Up*, the band Television's live cassette-only release on the ROIR label, recorded in 1978. I highly recommend it (along with practically the entire ROIR label catalog, by the way), but not as a source of soothing for a broken mind.

Some of the songs are long, but to me that day, they became endless. In fact, I had convinced myself that I was going to die if we ever turned the cassette off or let it stop playing. Over and over again it played through the night, all the way into Texas. Until, I guess, I fell asleep and everyone else in the van gave a quiet cheer, I assume.

I woke up at a truck stop in a little better shape. Still a bit scared and scarred. But functioning. I put on a pair of orange-tinted sunglasses that made everything look happier somehow, so I bought them. There are a few pic-tures out there of me wearing them, but they're mostly in black and white, so it's hard to tell how ridiculously orange they were.

Years later when I met Richard Lloyd from Televi-sion, I told him all about this episode and how "Little Johnny Jewel" simultaneously ripped me apart and held me together. He said, "That's nothing! I once spent a month convinced the radiator in my apartment was playing 'Over Under Sideways Down' by the Yardbirds!" And we laughed. And then we sighed. Both reminded we were lucky to be alive.

SCOTTISH ALARM

BEING AWAKENED BY AN INCREDIBLY LOUD FIRE ALARM mere minutes after dozing off in a large Scottish hotel.

Day three of a UK tour. Day three typically being the hardest day of jet lag effects for this traveler. So very, very tired.

Traipsing down carpeted hallways and staircases and vaguely registering an old building's musty odor mixed with what I can only describe as unfamiliar and un-American-smelling cleaning solutions.

Finding my bandmates and crewmates milling among the other guests in the "car park."

Too tired to talk.

Becoming slightly worried about, and a bit envious of, the members of our entourage who had apparently been able to sleep through the Scottish alarm's incessant nagging metallic pulse.

All clear, we're told. Go back to your rooms. Only a test. At two A.M.! A test.

Long line at the lone refrigerator-sized elevator taking two or three people (max) at a time back to their floors.

Giving up and climbing the four flights back to my room.

Alarm still going. Painfully loud.

Trying to sleep. So tired. Trying to ignore the seemingly broken alarm. Thinking maybe this is my life now. Squeezing my eyes shut. Holding pillows over my ears.

Something whispers in my ear: "Surrender."

I sit up on the edge of the bed and focus my attention on the sound, assuming it's the only thing there is to surrender to. Instead of struggling to NOT hear what is so inescapably there, I start to listen with intention.

What was once brutal, piercing, and painful slowly begins to reveal layers of tones and overtones. The chaos and noise reorders itself into something mesmerizing, beautiful, and complex.

I turn my head and swirls of harmonic nuance dance off of different surfaces in the room.

I turn my head again and swear I can hear the mirror on the closet adding a shimmering, clear top note.

I stand up and move around the room, and what was once a dull monotonous throbbing beat begins to reveal polyrhythms. I suppose thanks to a combination of the perception-altering duration and the very subtle reflections I'm beginning to grasp.

Now I'm wide-awake. I'm inspired.

I can't believe everything I'm hearing is real. I'm hallucinating grand soaring melodies now.

The hair on my arms begins to stand on end.

And then!

It's over. The alarm has stopped. It's silent.

I immediately feel a sense of mourning. I miss the sound. I begin to cry. I feel abandoned.

I sit back down on the edge of the bed.

Now I'm trying to hang on to the sound. I find myself trying to conjure a lingering ghost. I want to keep it with me always now.

The way one glimpse of a smile can carve a deep, indelible impression of a loved one's face to retrieve with the mind's eye—that's how I wish to be able to hear with my "mind's ear(s)" this transcendent aural gift again.

A gift I guess I gave myself by saying yes and surrendering.

The way one might say yes and surrender to the unimaginable power of the ocean. When the waves are crashing in and the only way to not be violently knocked over is to lie down and become a part of the ocean—part of the wave.

At this point in my life I had already developed a

piqued interest in John Cage, noise art, conceptual music . . . I had always been pretty curious when it comes to people making sounds. But I missed emotion and longed for sentiment in music I considered academic. I could not perceive a soul. Only a consciousness. Which, like I said, was exciting enough at that time in my life, so full of discovery and revelations.

Honestly, though, I didn't get it. Most experimental music was hard to feel any connection to.

Until the Scottish alarm explained it to me relentlessly.

The soul I perceived to be missing? My own.

4'33"

IT'S TEMPTING TO ILLUSTRATE THE POINT OF THIS composition—and perhaps the point of this book—by leaving this page blank. Issue a challenge to stare into the void, to journey within and accept that there is no "nothing." Pay attention! The music is YOU.

But I'm afraid, dear reader, that no matter how mild-mannered you may be, you, in turn, might find yourself tempted to slap me around a little bit should we ever cross paths. I would accept my beating with solemn dignity, knowing it to be just and fair. Anyway, it's too late now. I've already sullied the stillness of a blank page—trodden upon the freshly fallen snow, if you will . . . but what's that? You won't? Okay, never mind.

What I'm trying to say is . . . that blank page would have been a great way to get at what I'm trying to say. And since I'm remembering now that John Cage himself wrote a whole book called *Silence*, I'm not going to hesitate or feel bad about adding my own thoughts here. Because I doubt I would have ever thought about songs quite the way that I do without this bold, often misunderstood, even more often maligned, colossally important artistic gesture. This "song," along with "Cartridge Music" and the other experimental records I stumbled upon in the music library at Southern Illinois University Edwardsville while I wasn't going to my classes, changed my life.

My take on this music might not be the most accurate reading of its intentions academically. Honestly, I'm an inspired amateur. I came to this music like an early rock 'n' roll pioneer—by being dumbstruck with curiosity enough to feel compelled to find more at any cost. Picture me sneaking out of Bible studies class to sit in the bushes outside of a speakeasy, but instead of listening to some sweat-soaked rhythm and blues raunching and rolling across the bayou, I'm listening to a piano bench squeak and some coconuts being cracked open with a hot microphone.

ANCHORAGE

MY VERY FIRST BEST FRIEND GROWING UP WAS A GIRL (a tomboy, I was told) who lived six or seven houses away on the opposite side of the street. Whenever I was given permission to go play at her house, my mother would instruct me to cross the street directly in front of our house on my way there. And coming home, I was to wait until I was again directly in front of our house to cross.

In other words, she only wanted me to cross the street in front of our house. The subtext was clear to me—if I was going to get hit by a car, she wanted to watch. No. That's not fair. I guess it's more that she wanted to hear my cries should a car slam into my tiny body. Which is a totally normal motherly thing to desire.

But there was always a lot of confusing subtext with my mom. She was hit by a car on her ninth birthday—"I got a brand-new pair of pink leather cowboy boots and they had to cut them off of me." So there was that. There was also a lot of ominous hinting around that something wasn't right about the family that lived in the dirty white house directly opposite ours. They had a couple of kids my age, but my mom really discouraged me from making friends with them. She'd say stuff like "You can play in their front yard but don't you ever go in their backyard" and "I don't want you to EVER go in their house."

Subtle. Which was fine. They were destructive little shits and I loved my "girl" friend up the street—I mean my friend who happened to be a girl. And on top of that a tomboy . . . so definitely nothing weird going on. But there was something weird going on. Our peers, and the adults in our lives, were slowly but surely making things weird. The kids made fun of us for hanging out because of the whole "cooties" thing. Which honestly we were aware of, but we had chosen to roll the dice based on how much fun we were having. The adults were harder to read. They were obviously uncomfortable with us being so close and our hesitation to play with members of our own sex, but they never really voiced a reason for their concerns. Now, looking back, I think they were clearly worried that we were both gay. Wild times.

Sadly, over time the societal wedges we were facing worked to break us apart, and even sadder, I think, we eventually bought into the idea that there was something wrong with our being friends, to such a degree that, once apart, we kind of never looked back. We had been subtly coerced into being embarrassed about each other and it overpowered our innocence.

What does this have to do with Michelle Shocked and her song "Anchorage"? Not a lot, really. Or everything, maybe. I know of no other song more efficient at getting my eyes wet than this sweet song. I would guess it would have a perfect batting average if tunes were pitches and tears were singles and doubles. I can't even read the lyrics without choking up. And for the life of me, I could never quite understand why this particular song hits me so hard so consistently. It's a simple premise. Two friends grow apart and reconnect through the mail. The bulk of the lyrics are in the voice of Michelle's long-lost friend, bringing her up to date on the twists and turns her life has taken since they last spoke. Lovely stuff.

I think it's the profound air of forgiveness that gets me—the relief of having "walked across that burning bridge" and instead of being met with judgment and resentment, as feared, finding a warm embrace on the other side. After years and years of knowing this song and the power it has over my emotions and not knowing exactly why . . . after having given up on discovering why . . . I finally got my answer.

After a Wilco show in St. Louis in 2010, my aunt Gail walked up to me at the post-show meet-and-greet with a tall middle-aged woman in tow. "Do you know who this is?" she asked.

I wasn't sure I did at first. And then I saw her. The years melted away, and I was face-to-face with my long-lost, beloved very best girlfriend/friend who happens to be a girl. There she was. As we stood beaming at each other, she caught me up on her life. Married. Successful career as an artist. Tenured professor! And as we were winding down—as I was being propelled to the next group of meet-and-greeters—she pulled me in for a hug and said this in my ear: "I've paid attention. I'm so proud of you, my dear, dear courageous friend."

It might be the only time anyone has ever called me courageous to my face. But coming from someone who had only ever seen me as an ultra-sensitive little boy—a boy/friend who happened to be a boy—I accepted the appraisal as a succinct and deeply sincere way of telling me that she knows that, in spite of the outward appearance of having "made it," IT hasn't been easy. A statement of profound empathy. With just a handful of words, she had eased a pain she had witnessed from afar.

I felt whole again knowing we were good. Knowing that we never really stopped being friends—our affection for each other was well chosen and true. And that no one could ever take that away from us.

RENO, NEVADA

DRIVING INTO NEVADA FOR THE FIRST TIME EVER. Twenty extra dollars is agreed upon as a supplement to our per diem for our first foray into legal gambling. Topping a hill on a dark highway, bright lights on the horizon. Reno! We stop, gamble, lose.

Back in the van in under twenty minutes. Pass sign on highway—"Reno 8 miles." A $120 rapid injection into the Sparks, Nevada, economy.

(SITTIN' ON)
THE DOCK OF THE BAY

ARE THERE TOUGHER-SOUNDING OTIS REDDING SONGS?
For sure. Would I play this song for someone to bolster a
claim that he might have been the best soul singer of all
time? No. I would probably play you a live version of
"Try a Little Tenderness." But is this the single most immediately welcoming recording I've ever heard? Yes, I
believe it is.

I'm not sure I can even explain what this song does
to me or put into words how fundamentally this song
shaped my own perception of where one should aim
when writing a song. How high the bar is. It's a perfect
song. Effortless in its execution. Music that understands
itself completely. Betrays no need or desire to impress
beyond its own immaculately drawn conclusions. Saying clearly: Here are the waves. Listen. This is where we
will be for the next 2:47. Can you stop with all of your
overthinking for even just a moment?

It's like getting to hear a song write itself. The music feels like it's conjuring the words being sung. To me, this is the most magical type of song. Even coming out of a cheap AM radio car speaker, this song has the ability to wrap its own world around the listener. It creates a reality and gently surrounds you with it. Your ears see it. The listener is allowed in. To hear it is to be inside it. I am this song. You are this song. We all are.

And what a gift it is to have a song that can transport us somewhere else—take us away from our troubles, allow us a moment free of care . . . what more can a song do? This is the song that taught me all of that—whispered in my ear what I should aspire to. And when you hear the occasional whistled refrain in my own songs, I think I should let you know it's only there because Otis let me sit down on the dock beside him long enough to remember this: Thinking a lot can't really fix a whole hell of a lot. Sometimes, maybe you're better off whistling along with the waves for a while.

YOU ARE MY SUNSHINE

I'VE TRAVELED A LOT IN MY LIFE. ONE OF MY FAVOR-ite things to do when I'm given the opportunity to live a day of my life in a city far from my home is walk around. Sometimes I get to retrace my steps in places I've visited time and time again. The routine of being in a touring rock band has allowed me to get to know most of the major cities on a few continents by now. Occasionally, we go somewhere we haven't been, and I get even more excited to explore the new city on foot.

But I'm pretty content, in general, just getting to traipse around almost anywhere I find myself. I end up well acquainted with cool buildings, well-planned city centers, shaded river walks, great local restaurants . . . sometimes I'll even find myself taking a path I've taken before, just to revisit a particular tree in a park in Amsterdam, or a memorial beside a bike path in Portland, Maine, for some kids who died in a car crash.

I don't really think about it much. It just kind of happens. Like, "Oh, here's that leaning cemetery wall," or "I know where I am! If I keep walking in this direction there'll be a Victorian-era greenhouse on the left." I think this habit derived from an impulse to remind myself of where I've been. It's oddly comforting to think of something I've seen before and find out it still exists. Or see if it's changed or how much it's changed . . . and when I make the effort to check my memory of the past against the reality of my present, I often find myself staring at a rusty old bike lock I made a mental note of for some reason, and my brain will say something like, "Well, look at us, we're both still here, how 'bout that . . . you and me, you rusty old heart-shaped bike lock engraved with 'W.G. + F.S. Forever' hanging off of a fence on a bridge over the Rhine in Cologne. Good job, everyone!"

And then I head back to the hotel. One thing I discovered after many years of falling in love with weird specific bike locks, park trees, and "in memory of" stone benches around the world is that this attention to detail and piqued curiosity about my surroundings tends to dull considerably when I get home. I don't spend a lot of time walking around Chicago with the same sense of geological time spinning my mind toward the poetry of place. I enjoy getting out in the neighborhood and moving my body, but everything tends to blur a bit compared to my visits to less-familiar environs.

But occasionally I have these moments where it all hits me—the filter of familiarity that colors everything mundane falls from my eyes, and it's glorious again. I can see it all anew with the eyes that accompany me on my travels. I'll ask myself, "How is it possible to take all of this beauty for granted?" And when this happens, I always think of "You Are My Sunshine," and how there hasn't been a single moment of my life where this song felt unknown to me. I think about how long it took before I even thought of it as a song. And even longer before I contemplated the fact that someone had to have written it. An individual human person had made it up before anyone else had ever heard it.

How is it that this song can feel like it has always existed? Weren't we all just born to this song? Born to breathe this song like the air in our lungs? It's easy to overlook the blue in the sky, I guess. But it's important to come home and be reminded of how special it is. How does a song become a home? The same way houses do. People have to live in them. Life has to happen inside of them. Laughing, crying, shouting. A song is a home when it matters not at all who's singing it, young or old. It's built for any voice.

I work to never forget that it's also the greatest song ever written. There's no place like home.

RAUNCH HANDS

TRYING TO BOOK A BAND I LIKED CALLED THE RAUNCH Hands in the mideighties. Having no idea what I was doing, but calling the number on their record and hoping for the best. Reading the contract and equipment rider they sent me. Standard requests—money, a certain-size PA, cases of beer, pizza . . . stuff like that.

Whistling to myself in that distinct soft, descending way that says, "Um . . . not good." Realizing I had no idea what I was doing. Knowing they'd eventually figure out that I had no idea what I was doing. Which, judging by the lack of follow-up, happened fairly quickly.

31

I WILL ALWAYS
LOVE YOU

BUCKLE UP. BECAUSE WHAT I'M ABOUT TO SAY IS GO-
ing to provide some solid evidence to support the inar-
guable wisdom behind my never having the log-in
information for my own social media accounts. In fact,
for years now, I've adhered to a strict fail-safe protocol.
One that requires two keys to be entered and turned at
the same time before firing off a tweet or gram or tik
and/or tok.

At least that's how my "team" explains the process.
To be sure, at this very moment I'm sweating a bit. I'm
beginning to rethink the judiciousness of sharing what
I'm about to share. This opinion is controversial in what
was once a low-stakes kind of way. Decidedly. But there's
really no such thing as low-stakes in this era where
simply "liking" someone else's post, absentmindedly,
could lower your stock. It's an outrage economy and I
don't want anything to do with it. Still, ill-advised as it

may be, I think my long-held assessment of this song is worth talking about to serve a broader point.

I don't like this song. I think it stinks. Doesn't matter who sings it. It fries my nerves. If I had to single out one main offense, it'd be the AAAAAAAYYYYYY-EEEE-EYE part. I hate that. I think I have a tough time with extra syllables being added to long notes in general. Maybe because, as a singer, I'm not very good at it. That's definitely something I've learned over the years. People tend to diminish or dismiss stuff they're bad at. Musicians are hilariously consistent with this quirk. Now, when I'm talking shop with someone in a band (let's call him Johnny) and he says something absurd, like "No harmony vocal has ever improved a rock recording," I think to myself, "Johnny must suck at singing harmonies." So it's not like I don't get that I'm the problem here. I would never argue with someone about it. I'm sincerely happy for you if you're into it.

And it's not like I haven't tried. I have. Trust me, I've tried to like this song. Because other people love it, for one thing. And because I adore Dolly Parton. So, tell us, Jeff, why share such a negative view? Thank you, I'm glad you asked. Because I think it's okay to admit everything isn't made for you. Or that nothing is made for everyone. It's okay to not "get" something. I think it's important to feel free to dislike something other people lose their minds over. And because this is a book, and I'm not opening up the floor for debate. If this somehow irritates someone to the point they're compelled to "come at me" online, I won't care. I mean, I'm not going to see it. And even if I did, I wouldn't care enough to request the launch codes to respond.

So I might as well share this part, too . . .

One of the things people always marvel at about Dolly is that she wrote this song and "Jolene" in the same day. When I heard that for the first time, I thought to myself, "That's pretty impressive, but at least one of those two songs sucked." I possibly thought that so I could go back to feeling okay with myself as a hardworking songwriter.

So, just to be clear, I LOVE Dolly Parton! She's the best. Person, songwriter, singer. You name it, she's the best. All I'm saying is that "Jolene" was enough work for one day. Geez . . . why are you looking at me like that?

32

WANTED DEAD OR ALIVE

BON JOVI POSSESSES THE TYPE OF ARROGANCE THAT compels one to swing for the fences every time one steps to the plate (microphone). Every song is angling to be a world-changing anthem. It's completely alien to me.

So I reflexively reject everything Bon Jovi does. In fact, I hate it so much I'd like to retract my previous words advocating for allowing space for everyone to like what they like and despise what they despise. I was wrong. This song sucks and you should not like it. I guess I hadn't really contemplated this song thoroughly enough before I got all altruistic back there in that "I Will Always Love You" chapter.

SPIN SHOOT

DOING A COVER SHOOT FOR *SPIN* MAGAZINE IN THE late aughts with a bunch of other artists. It was their summer festival issue and the premise was that we were all in line for a porta-potty.

It became clear after a while that they were probably going to try for a foldout cover, because there were too many people to fit on the front page.

Publicists and managers were swooping in and demanding better placement for their artists. Everyone wanted to be in the back of the line because the porta-potty was going to be the punchline reveal when the cover was folded out.

I don't even remember how I ended up where I did.

But I did meet RZA!

"Your shoe's untied," he said, pointing down at my dirty white low-top Converse tennis shoes.

"Um . . . yeah, I know, thanks," I said.

"That your thing?" he queried.

"Yeah, kinda," I said. Truth being, I'd given up on trying to keep them tied.

"Cool." He nodded, adding, "That used to be my thing."

I love that guy. Might be the coolest I've ever felt.

33

BEFORE TONIGHT

THIS SONG BY THE BAND SOULED AMERICAN IS LIKELY the hardest track to find of any I've included here in this weird little book of love letters to songs. These guys were from Illinois. A little bit older band than Uncle Tupelo, but we traveled in the same "circuit," for lack of a word more accurate to describe the hodgepodge of Midwestern bars, clubs, and college cafeterias our tours were all comprised of.

I'd like to say I saw them play a lot, but owing to their habit of playing in near-total darkness, I'm not sure I ever really "saw" them at all. I definitely would have had trouble picking them out of a lineup. Matching each instrument and its player was certainly out of the question.

My wife, Susie, knew them all pretty well. The carved wooden animals that adorned the façade of her former club, Lounge Ax, were made by Jamey Barnard, who played drums in the band up until 1991. Jamey was also an insanely talented comic—possibly the best phone prankster of all time. His genius twist on the form being his ability to get people to call HIM. He'd lay traps by filling out the forms one used to find at checkout counters advertising too-good-to-be-true credit card deals and time-shares. (Again, it might be worth reminding people how most of the grifts and cons we associate with the internet predate the digital age and possibly even the printing press.)

Unwitting salespeople working in the dark ages of telemarketing would nonchalantly place the noose around their own necks by calling Jamey to discuss his possible interest in a cemetery plot, for example, and he'd record them reacting to absurd situations and characters he'd improvise on the spot. "I'm sorry if I sound frazzled, I'm just not sure what I'm going to do about all of this blood," or "I'd love to come by and talk in person . . . would you mind meeting at dawn?" Genius.

It's possible that the cassette recordings of the prank calls that Jamey gave Susie all those years back are easier to find online than some of Souled American's music. Worth looking for. We cherish our cassettes to the point of having had them backed up digitally more than once out of fear the tape will degrade beyond playability.

But this song doesn't have a whole lot to do with Jamey or prank calls. What I think first and foremost when I hear this song is the same thing I thought the first time I heard it—"I wish I could have written this."

It's the perfect combination of the metaphysical and the mundane—the cosmic and the commonplace. In general, it's about time. And how time moves at maddeningly inconsistent speeds dependent upon our moods and states of mind.

Even the way the song is performed contributes to the poetry. I'm always a sucker for a band all pointed in the same direction yet unconcerned with metronomic time. Like a group of friends walking toward the next bar—sometimes together, at other times in pairs, maybe someone is running to catch up after stopping to take a leak behind a dumpster, and then all together again. It's a beautiful feat to stretch musical time like that. Maybe a little undervalued in western music. It takes a lot of trust in each other as a band to allow a song to just happen as opposed to being performed.

It's an intimate act to agree upon, not being perfect. I'm moved by it every time. And as a set of lyrics, it's hard for me to resist quoting the entire song. But I'll restrain myself and just share this, which is what lies at its heart. And has been on my mind for decades now . . .

A song before a voice
A chance before a choice
A lamp before a light

Stuck with today
Before tonight
A spool before a wind
A found after a find
A youth before a past
At least before . . .
At last

34

SHOTGUN

WHEN MY WIFE, SUSIE, AND I WERE MARRIED, ON A miserably hot August evening in 1995, she was unmistakably pregnant, with five and a half months' worth of baby Spencer growing inside of her body. The ceremony was held in Chicago at the rock club she co-owned with her partner, Julia, on Lincoln Avenue, across from the Biograph Theater and the alley next to it where John Dillinger was killed after being ratted out by another moviegoer or his date, "the lady in red," depending on whom you ask.

But that night, *Nine Months* was the movie being advertised on the theater's marquee. It was a fun wedding. Some family attended. My dad brought his own cooler of beer from downstate, even though we had assured him we had him covered, Lounge Ax being a bar and all. But most of our guests were our friends from the local music community we loved so much and felt so connected to. And they loved us enough to surprise us with a ragtag marching band to march us down the "aisle." If you were in a band in Chicago in the midnineties and had a horn or a snare drum lying around, there's a good chance you were at our wedding. Thank you.

Our friend Lana, an extraordinarily gifted cocktail waitress ordained by the Universal Life Church, officiated. Susie and I stood on the stage, said our vows, and stepped on a glass (tradition!). And when the kick-ass rhythm and soul band we had hired for the party joined in, they played the only truly obvious song we could have requested if we'd thought about it: "Shotgun," by Junior Walker and the All Stars.

Now, don't get me wrong—there are a lot of ways the idea of a "shotgun wedding" is uncool. And if we were more uptight, we might have felt the need to set the record straight. Truth is, I wasn't being coerced to "make it official" and marry Susie. In fact, I felt like I was lucky she wanted to marry me at all. If you knew me at the time, it would have been hard to imagine what she thought she was getting in the bargain. But on the other hand, it was a funny song to play, and everyone got a big kick out of it. She was pregnant, after all.

So this song comes up a lot in our house. When we get to talking with new friends or neighbors about how we got together, I always hear this in my head . . .

Shotgun!
Shoot him 'fore he run now

ROCK CLUB GHOST SHIP

EARLY NINETIES. ARRIVING FOR SOUND CHECK IN Houston at an unlocked venue only to find it completely vacant and with the eerie sense that all humans, staff and clientele alike, who were once here have now vanished. Cigarettes smoldering, blurry melting iced cocktails sweating on the bar—like some kind of underground rock club ghost ship.

Following the unmistakable hollow gurgling sound of a massive bong hit, leading us to the corner perch of what appears to be the venue's lone survivor—the house sound man.

Being mesmerized by the absolutely Cheech-ian (or possibly Chong-ian) cloud of smoke emanating from and blotting out the face of the house "sound dude" as he informs us that the PA we are currently supposed to be sound checking with has been lent to a friend and will "probably" be back around midnight. He suggests we go "chill out at Denny's" and come back at midnight. The xeroxed flyers in the entryway say "Uncle Tupelo 10 P.M."

Starting our set at two A.M. Five attendees. No paying customers. Just the band that brought the PA back and the sound dude.

35

THE WEIGHT

EVERYBODY KNOWS AND LOVES THIS SONG. OR AT least every musician I've ever met. Although I'm ashamed to admit I once moderated my high opinion of the Band, and this song in particular, because of a Robert Crumb interview where he used "The Weight" as an example of how ridiculous and corny his musical contemporaries were. He could have just said he strongly preferred Dixieland jazz and early string band 78s, but he's en-titled to his opinion.

The shameful part is how it stuck in my head for so long. And because I liked his art and shared with him an affinity for early recordings and the unparalleled excite-ment of getting to hear new forms in their infancy, I had a period where I kind of agreed with him. Looking at the Band's album jackets, I'd think to myself, "Look at these carpetbagging Canucks posing like they just robbed the Southern Pacific mail train, with their bushy beards and waistcoats . . . pfff!"

Now, some of you who've been following my career might be thinking, "Um, excuse me, Jeff, but I seem to recall you spending a good portion of your public life standing underneath hats and singing through a beard." I hear you. It's a weird disconnect. But it doesn't need to make sense. Because it's true. I have often donned and appropriated the styles of those whose authenticity I found suspect. I'm sure if I had the energy for such a topic I could rationalize my sartorial choices as being an extension of my desire to simultaneously embrace and subvert traditional American folk music forms. But in doing so I would sound like an asshole. So let's just agree that it's hard to find stuff to wear onstage. Especially when you aren't particularly interested in the showbiz side of things. So somebody gives you a hat and you put it on, and someone else, maybe a publicist or someone in your band, tells you that you "look good" and says, "Man, you should rock that onstage." And before you know it, you're standing at a microphone years later looking out at an audience full of guys wearing "your" hat.

Let's get back to "The Weight," shall we?

Eventually I realized R. Crumb was kind of a creep for being so closed-minded about rock music, and maybe even kind of a creep in general. So I was able to reclaim both the Band and "The Weight" with unabashed fervor.

Of course, the other element that I've failed to

mention—the one performance most responsible for making the song unassailable to myself and almost every musician I've ever met—is the movie *The Last Waltz*'s rendition with the Staple Singers. As great as the original studio recording of this song is, it doesn't have Mavis Staples. I've watched it a thousand times and I still can't understand the full ramifications of what it tells us about Mavis's singular talent. Pure commitment, entirely free of pretense, a range of emotions on display in one line that surpasses what most other singers could summon up in an entire career . . . and above all else, the thing I think it's impossible to find more of in any other footage of any other artist: joy.

With this one sublime performance, Mavis goes beyond just inhabiting a song, as all other musicians strive to do. She inhabits herself—her own skin—so completely, so free of judgment, so visibly generous in her spirit, that to see it is to be changed. It made such an impression on me that when we met years later I had to hide my shock that she wasn't, as I had pictured her, nine feet tall. If humanity at some point in the future is ever put on trial before a galactic body, I hope this footage still exists, because I can think of nothing more redeeming for all of us than to witness Mavis in all her glory.

36

WILL YOU LOVE ME TOMORROW

LIKE SO MANY OF MY OTHER FAVORITE SONGWRITERS I've been writing about, Carole King could easily have been the sole focus of this book if all I wanted to discuss was songcraft. Picking fifty of her songs would have been a piece of cake. And in terms of sharing what I've learned from other songwriters just by listening to their records, I can't think of anyone more important to me.

But in writing this, I'm trying to get at something beyond the contributions made by the songwriters themselves. I'm much more fascinated by the blurry area between a song and the mind that receives it, puts it back together in a shape that fits their own life, and allows the heart to take ownership. In my case I have the added mystery of how being a singer of other people's songs in front of an audience becomes so deeply personal, and leaves me feeling more exposed than even the most emotionally naked of my own songs.

There was a period in my life, back in the early Wilco days, when singing this song as an encore—a ballad that I would often deliver lying on my back while being held aloft and passed by the outstretched arms of fans, crowd surfing in slow motion—felt like I was being as honest as I could ever be with an audience. Will you still love me tomorrow? All of you. Will you? Because this night is forever to me. I can feel you . . . I sense you mean it right now in this moment . . . I can allow myself to trust you. But you're going to move on, aren't you?

It's a hard thing to admit sometimes as performers, but we need you. And I wouldn't be within a thousand feet of a stage if I didn't desperately want to feel this connection. I want to be seen. I want to feel special. But you're seeing other bands, aren't you?

As ridiculous as that all sounds, it's a true revelation of an internal dialogue that is always happening just below the surface of any song I'm singing. Singing "Will You Love Me Tomorrow" back in the day was my effort to come clean. I'm in love with you people out there listening. Please don't hurt me.

GERMAN BURGER KING

LEAVING A BRIEFCASE CONTAINING OUR ENTIRE TOUR'S net income under a table at a truck stop Burger King in Germany. Discovering this fact an hour after we'd gotten back on the autobahn.

Returning two hours after we had left and finding it in the exact same spot where we left it. Eating again.

37

FREE BIRD

AS I WRITE THESE WORDS IN 2023, IT FEELS OBVIOUS to me that what I'm about to say should be unnecessary. Alas, dear reader, it remains a scourge that must be addressed. Here goes: Yelling "Free Bird" in any context is dumb. It's not clever or funny. It makes YOU look bad. Since about 1989 everyone who has participated in this little stunt has woken up the next morning ruing the decision to yell "Free Bird." I'm not trying to be mean. Don't do it. Save yourself.

My life onstage has been peppered every step of the way by this inane occurrence. Setting aside the undue burden this has placed on my life, the world "Free Bird" created for itself is exactly what this book is about.

Sometimes, the life a song takes on when unleashed upon a chaotic society can become monstrous. Lynyrd Skynyrd didn't want this. They wrote an ode to restless liberty (and shameless romantic conquest, perhaps). And now look at it . . . it's a punch line to the worst joke on earth. The music side of the song was stripped and sold for parts. The title alone stands. A proto-meme. Hearing it from the stage or audience is as close to Rickrolling as we could get back in the pre–World Wide Web before-times.

Now that Rickrolling itself has passed its sell-by date, I feel like everyone should just know not to request "Free Bird." Sadly, I can feel my words falling on deaf ears. And I fear only draconian measures like immediate re-movals and lifetime venue bans could once and for all set us all free from this vibe-killing menace. We've trav-eled far past the "they know not what they do" plea for leniency. So I'll just have to beg you, please, don't do it.

Do, however, throw on "Free Bird"—the actual song, yes—sometime and marvel at the truly spectacular guitar interplay that comes close to fully erasing the pathetic self-aggrandizing lyrics from the front half, the ballad half of the song. Pee-wee Herman telling Dottie not to fall in love with him because he's "a loner, a rebel" was more convincing. Geez. Now I want to hear it!

38

THE STAR-SPANGLED BANNER

"NO WAY, THANK YOU, BUT NO." THAT'S WHAT I SAID without hesitation when my next-door neighbor asked me over our backyard fence if I'd ever be interested in singing the national anthem at a sporting event.

He wasn't just asking idly; he happened to be an employee of one of the major sports teams in Chicago. Kind of high up, even. So he was a guy who could make it happen. We were friends. Still are, even though he and his awesome wife and dogs moved out of the city a few years ago. But I still think it hurt his feelings when I elaborated by telling him that I think it's a terrible song. "It's militaristic, and even if I liked it, it's too hard for a guy like me to sing.

"If they ever change the national anthem to something more reasonable, hit me up," I added as he clapped his golden retriever up to his porch to go back inside.

With hindsight, I can see that I handled the question tactlessly.

However, I stand by it. The idea of America—the promise of these United States—deserves better than a crappy battle song. If it were up to me, I think I'd try to sell everyone on the idea of something with a wordless melody everyone can sing. Like the riff from "Seven Nation Army," but I guess that might conjure up the same sort of "Fuck you, world" we were trying to avoid.

I know!

Stevie Wonder is still alive; let's get him to write us a celestial anthem that glows in the dark. Before it's too late.

THE *MARY* F***ING *CELESTE*

WALKING AROUND INSIDE THE WARNER BROS. BUILD-
ing in Burbank, California, with my then manager
looking for someone who could direct us to the head of
A&R's office. Realizing that we strolled right in without
the usual security stop and hadn't seen a single person
since entering. Beginning to notice half-eaten sandwiches
on desks and other odd evidence that people had left in
some type of hurry. Going floor to floor, shouting hello
up and down hallways—nothing. The *Mary* fucking *Ce-
leste*. Giving up and heading toward the exits. Two security guards informing us the building was about to be
declared "all clear" after a bomb threat.

Pre-9/11.

Learning that bomb threats against record label HQs
were fairly common. Common enough that, upon threat
notification, everyone we were supposed to meet had
calmly walked over to the commissary on the WB lot for

lunch. Not one person thought they should try to get ahold of the Wilco guy and give him a heads-up?

Daydreaming about how high on the list of crazy rock-related deaths my demise would have ranked had an actual bombing of the WB building occurred with the only victims being myself and my manager.

Not to mention the conspiracy theories that would form.

I mean, I wasn't even scheduled to perform. Had just flown in that morning for a meeting about my "career." Why was I there? Was it a setup? Where was security?

Meeting a bust.

39

RADIO FREE EUROPE

WHEN I COME ACROSS EARLY R.E.M. SONGS IN THE wild now—a restaurant playlist, the occasional hip elevator—they hit me the way a vague early childhood sense memory might. Like how a musty smell might take you back to your grandparents' root cellar—no specifics attached, just a bodily reminder that you were also you, alive, in the past and that you inhabited spaces you no longer have access to without the gentle coaxing of a certain type of light or smell.

The crazy thing is, R.E.M. songs started out this way, at least for me. Hearing them for the first time felt like my earlier thoughts and feelings were being recollected. For kids like me and my friends, it was disorienting and intoxicating to have new music that felt somehow old. Songs that radiated sincerity yet gave only a lip of soft clay as a foothold for meaning.

These were our thoughts—our confused internal

dialogues—our wild curiosity, muffled by the slight em-
barrassment of our own earnestness being sung back to
us. At the time it didn't even feel like the band themselves knew what to make of it all. And their bewilder-
ment fed our belief in them. Listening to them was an
act that felt on equal footing with their intent. The general laws of capitalism usurped by a gift economy where
giving was getting and vice versa, but "money" wasn't
part of the equation.

Of course, it was all a bit of a youthful fantasy. Like
everyone else, R.E.M. wanted hits, and wanted to get
paid. And, of course, they deserved to be paid. But that
never stopped me from holding deep and cherishing the
idea that music belongs to both sides, the creator and the
listener. Feeling ownership of music you didn't make
through the simple act of investing yourself into it will
always be more real to me than whatever goes on at the
New York Stock Exchange.

The main difference? You can't put a price on it.

40

I'M AGAINST IT

AS I GET OLDER, I'M FINDING IT HARDER AND HARDER to comprehend how a miracle like the Ramones happens. How are they real? How is it that something like the Ramones ever occurred outside of someone's imagination? The mystery deepens when you take in the fact that they're all gone. Every original "Ramone" has now shed this mortal coil. If I think about it too much, I start to find the argument for the existence of a higher power more compelling. Maybe there is a GOD!

Oddly enough, the evolutionary theories regarding randomness, genetic mutation, and natural selection also get bolstered by contemplating my favorite band, ever, from Queens. Either explanation—god or spontaneous mutation—feels weak on its own. Together, the normally opposing concepts start to make sense.

The truth is, I should stop thinking so hard. I'll never

understand. I should just say "What the FUCK?!" and move on. You know, "let the mystery be," as Iris De-Ment says in one of my favorite songs ever. What I should focus on is my good fortune. Thank my lucky stars I walked the earth at the same time as these weirdos.

As for the songs themselves, it's hard to pick just one. And in a way, individually, they don't matter. Favorites aside, what matters is the travail—the discipline and gargantuan levels of self-possession required to create not just a "band" with "songs" but to invent a world where every gesture is iconic. Everything from white canvas sneakers and leather jackets to how a song gets counted in onstage is, ostensibly, a fully considered addition to the big picture. All contours clearly defined— and yet, artistic choices seemingly spontaneous and blind, i.e., not "choices" at all. Which also makes plain some unmistakable genius at work—sharp, deliberate, and permanent.

All of this is to say I ADORE the Ramones. If I haven't heard them for a while, tears of joy shoot out of my eyes like windshield wiper fluid when we're re-united.

This song? "I'm Against It"? Well . . . I'm for it. The lesson learned from having this song in my life is precious to me. We CAN have joy and OWN our alienation at the same time. These lyrics are funny and dumb, but to me they're as profound as any other proper poetry I've ever met. The way I see it, at some point saying what you hate transcends negativity—it becomes liberating. It's "punk" rock math. A thousand no's adds up to one big fucking YES!

COACHELLA

FIRST FEW DAYS IN REHAB. I WAS A BASKET CASE. STRUG-gling with full-blown panic attacks all day long. Just really wiped out, and not thinking about being a musician. And certainly not thinking that anybody who worked at this hospital knew who I was or had any interest in what I was doing.

Young guy on the night shift, coming into my room and asking, "I was just curious, are you guys still playing Coachella?"

"What do you think?"

"My friends and I are going, I was just curious if you were still going . . ."

"I'm in the hospital . . ."

We did cancel.

41

BIZCOCHITO

I WISH I'D TAKEN SPANISH WHEN I WAS IN SCHOOL. Most kids I knew in high school did. A few took German. But I chose French, for some reason that eludes me to this day. Not that it would have mattered. Had I taken Spanish, I'm sure I would have been just as good at not learning that language as any other. Let's just say, cher lecteur, mon français c'est de la merde!

Now, after traveling quite a bit in Europe I can generally grasp enough of what's being spoken around me to grok the gist. But I still get sad that I wasn't able to apply myself to learning at least one other language. And when I first heard Rosalía's music, that agonizing sense that I had missed out on some precious life-enhancing knowledge by neglecting to grow another tongue hit me harder than ever.

However, being on the outside looking in didn't stop me from falling in love with Rosalía's voice and her crazy run of artistic quantum leaps. So I kept listening. And listening. And listening. And before long I started noticing something profound happening. I started to believe I could understand what she was saying most, if not all, of the time. Not literally. Emotionally.

It then shocked me when I started googling English translations of her lyrics and realizing my theory—the possible wishful thinking of a mono-language dope—could hold water. I was more than just in the general ballpark based on half-understood Spanish phrases sneaking through the mix. I wasn't just grabbing on to fragments and putting together a plausible story. I could actually hear the look on her face. I could see the man she was singing to—pinpoint the heartache to a specific moment in her life.

In this song—way before I ever checked out the literal translation—I had perfectly understood the scope of how succinctly she could tell someone who might dare to underestimate her to back the fuck off. Now, I understand what you might be thinking: "That's not that impressive, all songs create meaning outside of directly understood lyrics. Most of us are clearly performing these feats of listening without trying to make ourselves out to be some kind of genius listener."

To which I say, I get it. I agree. But my point isn't that it's just me and my well-honed ears unlocking the "Rosalía stone." I'm saying that, yes, it's typical for musical keys and vocal inflections, etc., to shape what we take away from a song—that's a fact. But I'm also arguing that no one on earth has ever sung that extra layer of nonlanguage meaning as virtuosically and clearly at the same time. The lyrics themselves are snotty, revealing, playful, aggressive, lurid, innocent, funny, morbid, joyous, defiant . . . just full to the brim with life.

But the ability to sing two languages at once, one inside of the other, is where she makes the case for herself as a generational talent. It reminds me of the recent discoveries in how a bird's song is perceived by other birds. Which has revealed that while we're hearing the simple "whippoorwill" of a whippoorwill, for example, another whippoorwill is able to discern massive amounts of microtonal variation imparting different types of information within the same song.

I can't explain it further, but it makes sense to me. It also makes sense to me that Rosalía's first discipline was flamenco (in which she has a master's degree). And while I can't claim to understand all of the implications of why that particular starting point makes perfect sense, I do know that it's a folk tradition that employs what appear to be microscopically calibrated gestures and variances to tell the most dazzling, passionate story one can pull from oneself.

On top of all of this top-tier vocal talent and emotional intelligence, Rosalía is forging a path for herself artistically in a way that looks positively Dylan-esque to a Dylan-obsessed fellow like myself. How's that for taking something so clearly belonging to the world at large and grinding it through the old-white-guy lens? But there really are parallels. Taking something old and making it sound modern is nothing new. She's done that. Dylan did that.

But beyond that, to transform timeworn musical forms into shapes that sound like a new type of future, and do so repeatedly and seemingly at will, deserves recognition alongside people like Miles Davis and Picasso.

In fact, I'd be willing to bet that at some point in the future, those iconoclasts might end up being referred to as the Rosalías of their time. The major difference, of course, being that she's an enormous international pop star already. No critical reevaluation of Rosalía's work will be necessary for the masses to catch up. She somehow manages to wrap all of her bold moves and innovations inside utterly irresistible pop shapes. If she were a painter, I would say at some point she stopped painting on canvas and just started replacing everyone's eyes with a new type of eye. Eyes designed for the invisible colors at the edges of the rainbow. When Rosalía sings, life looks and sounds different. Everything is a new, previously unexplored possibility.

Admittedly, I could have picked another song to talk about. Perhaps one that better illustrates the direct lineage to the folk tradition she has emerged from. But this song makes me so goddamn happy I didn't want to pass up a chance to put it in front of someone new. Besides, you should be listening to all of what she has to offer anyway. Come get your new eyes!

42

THE BEATLES

THIS IS THE ONLY BAND I'M GOING TO WRITE ABOUT without picking a single song. And you know why, don't you? Because it's impossible. On top of the fact that I've formed a deep personal relationship with their entire catalog, they're the only band I can feel 100 percent certain that anyone who might pick up this book has formed some opinion of through their own experience.

Everyone loves the Beatles. Even people who hate the Beatles know they should love them, and what they're reacting to negatively isn't the actual Beatles—it's their ubiquitousness, their largeness. Or maybe one's own feeling of having had them foisted upon them by everyone. If someone tries to tell you that the Beatles were actually bad at music, or that they objectively think they sucked, you're talking to a person without ears or a heart or a mind or possibly even a BODY! You should run from that miserable demon before they make you sick.

All you need to do to understand the universal appeal of the Beatles is find yourself in the same room as a kid (infant on up) hearing them for the first time. It's instantly clear to them—"This is great, where have you been keeping this stuff?!" Like how we managed to not let Spencer have any sugar until we broke down on his first birthday and bought him a cake. I swear, literally one second after a single molecule of chocolate icing reached his tongue, his face changed into a look that we had never seen before. A face I can only describe as possessed . . . but possession by way of some cute version of Satan, or maybe the "Trix are for kids" rabbit. While we sat paralyzed by his expression, he immediately lunged for the cake and hugged it to his chest. You know . . . like the Beatles. You get it. I'm not going to waste any more of your time. Go enjoy your own connection to the Fab Four.

I will say that having the Beatles in the world can feel pretty daunting as a musician. Everyone doing what I do kind of knows the world already has the Beatles. It's incredibly unlikely any of us will get anywhere close to that kind of impact. Culturally, that is. Musically, they're the opposite. They're a shining beacon for everyone to steer toward if you choose to aim your art outward, openly giving and reaching for love. The scale of the magical structure they built is unattainable, but the sandbox is still full of the same sand—we're all allowed to build with the same material. And we've even been encouraged, by them, to think in new shapes.

One of the most pivotal moments in my life as a musician was when the *Beatles Anthology* series was released. At the time, there was little out there to suggest anything other than polished, visionary record-making from the Beatles. They weren't a band that had been bootlegged nearly as much as a lot of other artists. I suspected and craved confirmation that they had to have sounded human (bad, or at least not perfect) at some point in the process of album-making. So when these collections of demos, early takes, rough mixes, and outtakes came out, I felt I'd been handed a treasure map. A schematic of love, clear and readable enough to reverse-engineer any type of tune. Did "Strawberry Fields" always sound like music made by an underwater candy orchestra? Why, no. Here you can listen to it how it was written. Like a normal song strummed on an acoustic guitar. What about "Helter Skelter"? That must have just been lightning striking, right? First take, perhaps? Visionary proto-metal, quantum-leap guitar onslaughts like that must be born of a clear bolt out of the blue. Nope. Just a tepid blues trudge here. Fascinating nonetheless, because YOU know they're onto something, even though they don't quite sound like they'll ever get there.

It's truly hard to overstate how important it was to be given the validation of knowing that even the Beatles struggled, made wrong turns, changed course, and ultimately surrendered to each unsure moment as an invitation to swim in a starlit sky of possibility. I was given permission to sound bad on my way to sounding great by these records. Bad with gusto and an unabashed joyful wonder. No one looks inside and discovers only diamonds and pearls. If art is at least in part an act of discovery, you might as well learn how to enjoy getting lost, too.

ABBEY ROAD

BEING TOLD BY THE TICKET AGENT AT O'HARE THAT my passport had expired mere days before the date on my ticket. Abbey Road mastering session set to begin in eighteen hours.

Going straight from O'Hare to the Federal Building downtown to get in line for an expedited passport renewal. *Yankee Hotel Foxtrot* master tapes in tow.

After six hours downtown, heading back to O'Hare with shiny new expedited miracle passport to catch the overnight flight to London Heathrow.

Taking a black cab directly from Heathrow to Abbey Road. Somehow arriving only an hour late.

Good news—being sort of on time with *YHF* reels intact.

Bad news—cabin pressure on the flight rendered me deaf in my right ear. Miserable and frustrated.

Meeting and informing mastering engineer Steve

Rooke of my monophonic hearing situation. "Steve, I'm afraid I won't be of much value today. I can only hear out of my left ear."

"Well, Jeff, we should be fine, because I can only hear with my right ear. Let's sit side by side and between us we'll have a good pair of ears," Steve said dryly.

As I began to scoot my chair next to his at the mixing desk to create the desired stereophonic pair of ears, I heard what he had said again in my mind—this time in an exaggerated "Beatles" voice. Oh, I get it. A joke as dry as a day-old scone.

Ahhhh . . . the British.

Abbey Road!

43

CLOSE MY EYES

I FEEL LIKE I'VE TALKED A LOT, HERE AND ELSEWHERE, about how much stock I put in the idea that almost all songs function in a way that consoles the listener with a brief but vital companionship. In essence taking the place of another human in the room—another consciousness filling the void of isolation. It's a tender relationship regardless of a song's musical nature. From the bleakest black metal to the sweetest pop confection. The power to embrace the lonely is always at the heart of the bargain.

I still believe that to be a rock-solid truth, but I also think that there's an equally important piece of humanity that some songs are uniquely efficient at teaching us about: empathy. It's kind of the same idea turned on its head, really. Instead of the listener's loneliness being acknowledged and erased, some songs remind us that there are other people out there NOT like us, going through things we can't fathom.

They need us, too—they deserve to be seen and we should work to understand them. The amazing thing is, some songs can perform this beautiful task without our even knowing or buying into the effort consciously. Here's how I think that works—we sing along in our heads, and when a song is in the first person, our minds hear us say "I" a lot. Now, I'm not sure if you are aware of this, but the "I" word carries a ton of fucking weight in our psyches. I picture anthropomorphized brain cells scrambling—"Is he singing about us! When did this happen?!? Let's get some images together ASAP. Feelings?! You MF-ers up?!? There we go. Crying now."

So it just sort of happens, I think. We know it's not us. But some part of who we are identifies it as "us," because we just experienced it the only way we know how—with access to only one consciousness. Because we have no choice. We're all kind of locked inside of ourselves with only one channel to watch. Everything is us. But some songs have the ability to sneak someone else's point of view past the well-guarded gates of our egos. And I think that how little our own intent matters makes it more powerful—we don't have to say to ourselves, "I'm going to work on identifying with a closeted gay teenager from Iowa today." But a song like "Close My Eyes" by Arthur Russell not only puts us in someone else's shoes, it bends down and ties them for us.

Arthur Russell wrote this song sometime in the eighties but it wasn't released until 2008, long after his death in 1992. It's a simple country-folk song just about at the opposite end of the spectrum from the experimental cello-driven dance music Russell was more well-known for.

Initially, I was sucker-punched by the song's warmth and charm compared to the icier music I was expecting. But it wasn't long before the words began seeping in—setting up shop. Putting me many steps closer to understanding what it feels like to be a closeted gay teenager growing up in rural Iowa. Closer to seeing through his eyes. And my having been taught to see this way made the song more human. Which has a funny way of making the "other" more human to me forever. Both of us now safer from my former ignorance and misunderstanding.

I close my eyes and listen
To hear the corn come out
Don't you hear the stars they glisten
As we go in and out
Down where the trees grow together
And the western path comes to an end
See the sign it says clear weather
I'll meet you tonight, my friend
Will the corn be growing a little tonight
As I wait in the fields for you
Who knows what grows in the morning light
When we can feel the watery dew

I just can't be there with no other
I know those hills will be true
Away from my sister and brother
Down through the grasses so new
The air is sweet and steady
And flowers bloom out of sight
I know the sky is ready
Come meet me down here tonight
Will the corn be growing a little tonight
As I wait in the fields for you
Who knows what grows in the morning light
As we can feel the watery dew

44

HAPPY BIRTHDAY

I SHOULD LOVE THIS SONG.

Reason 1: It's the ultimate folk song in that it's almost never sung in a formal setting. No one goes to a recital to see a guy in a tux sing "Happy Birthday." "Until you've heard Pavarotti sing it, you'll never truly appreciate it. By the time he got to the 'You belong in a zoo' part I had tears streaming down my cheeks." Outside of the waitstaff at TGI Fridays, no one gets paid to sing "Happy Birthday."

Reason 2: Obviously there are no other contenders for a song more often sung to us on joyous occasions. Ditto for songs sung to loved ones on their special day.

The sad truth is, I'm pretty ambivalent about this song. I'd even go so far as to say that I actively disdain singing it more often than not. I think things started to shift for me about the same time I started making records and being a musician began to be more legitimate in the eyes of my extended family members. Which is when I began to notice people looking at me as we gathered around the candle glow of a birthday cake and expecting me to "wow" them with my vocal chops. "Why isn't he leading us?" and "I can barely hear him, this is how he makes a living?" and "Doesn't seem like he knows the words" are just a few of the things I've suspected people were thinking.

I'm not alone, though. I have a nephew who struggles with the sensory overload of his relatives breaking out into song and ruining a perfectly enticing cake experience. He had grown to hate the song so much that on other family birthdays, we give his mom and dad enough of a heads-up to allow them to escort him out of earshot. One year on Susie's birthday, even being taken to the farthest corner of our backyard wasn't enough to prevent the mirthful strains of "Happy Birthday" from reaching his ears and causing a fairly major meltdown.

After some backroom counseling, he regained his composure enough to rejoin us at the table. At which point he calmly announced that he had something very important to share as he bit into his first bite of cake: "I hate all of you." Amen. Sometimes it takes someone brave enough to tell us the truth.

BANANA PANCAKE RECIPE

LATE NINETIES. BEING ASKED TO GO TO JOHN CALE'S home to write with him. Knocking on his door. Expecting him to be in black and white like the back cover of a Velvet Underground album. Being jarred by the man in shorts and a neon-pink tank top answering the door. John Cale in color. His idea—let's put a recipe to music.

Me, smart person, suggesting the banana pancake recipe located near the front of *Gravity's Rainbow*. Which I was familiar with because it fell within the zone of pages I had read before eventually giving up on the rest of the book, something that happened at least seven or eight times. Playing acoustic guitar while John Cale read aloud with his Welsh accent, which was totally familiar to me from his records, "melt in the skillet. Peel more bananas, slice lengthwise . . ."

Still feeling like this is more made up or dreamed than real. No evidence it ever happened . . . but it did.

45

LOVE LIKE A WIRE

HAVE YOU EVER HEARD A CONSTANT BUZZING BACK-ground radiation of regret whispering in your ear, saying, "You blew it"? Boy, I sure have.

In this case, I have a very particular type of ruing hanging around taunting me—the kind where you thought you had all the time in the world to tell someone what they mean to you, and then you blink, and they're gone. Gone-forever gone. Like dead gone.

It's a painful lesson. And I guess it's a pretty hard one to avoid. But that doesn't stop me from feeling awful about never telling Diane Izzo how great she was. I had chances—not a lot of them, but more than one would need to just say "Dang, you write great songs." If I had been listening closer, giving her the amount of undivided attention she deserved, I might have been able to hear her sing this song in person.

But I didn't. I took her for granted. We swam in the

same circles—played shows together, even. So, I had opportunities, before she died, to see her as she was: a gifted songwriter and great human. She also happened to write one of my favorite songs of all time, "Love Like a Wire." Which makes this part even more difficult to hear—believe it or not, the song was never officially recorded and released. So now I also regret writing about a song you can't go and listen to. If you search for it online, you'll probably find some clips of me singing it. But that's it.

I only know of this song because after she died, her husband was working tirelessly to put together a tribute record of other artists doing her songs. Through various folks we have in common, I was handed a rough demo of Diane's version as a guide for the version I was asked to contribute. Hearing her sing these lyrics for the first time—through layers of static and across years of warped space and time—she sounded so alive. Maybe even more alive than me in the moment. Because you have to be really alive to sing something like this . . .

> Climb out onto my burning rope
> If they ask, you can say it was true love
> If they ask, you can say you're the only one who bows
>   to love

Sadly, her husband also passed away before he was able to finish his project, and none of the tracks he was lovingly assembling for the album in her memory have been released. I have some close friends working on ways to remedy that situation.

In the meantime, I've been working on not holding back in the moment. Ask any band that's toured with us in the last ten years or so. I think I freak a lot of them out when they get offstage, showering them with praise and encouragement. I mean it, too. It's such an honor to be a witness to someone else's art. Letting them know that all of the heart and soul they've put into their work is bright and visible is the least I can do.

I love getting to know other musicians, and it's weird to admit, but a lot of them care about my caring about them. I know they hear me and what I say is meaningful. Diane Izzo taught me to give it all up—every ounce of love. Before it's too late.

46

I LOVE YOU

AS THE SONGS I'M EXCITED TO WRITE ABOUT GET closer and closer to the present moment, I'm finding them more difficult to write about. Not because I think there's anything lacking. In my opinion there are always quality songs being written. And imparting my judgment, quality-wise, isn't even the main point of these chapters. This book is about how much we all can bring to a song as listeners—how we can make a bad song profound, dance to a song about death, hate a song because it "belongs" to a version of ourselves we'd rather not dwell upon or, worse yet, was a favorite of someone we'd rather not think about.

All of these things take time. The way it takes time to break in a new pair of jeans or new pair of shoes. Which is the best explanation I can come up with for why newly released music gets harder to talk about using the premise of this book. It's also a good explanation for why a lot of people start to believe that music just isn't as good as it was when they were younger. Like it's a real mystery why something you might overhear coming out of some kid's phone on a beach just doesn't stack up against the songs you listened to a thousand times a day, on headphones, at THE specific moment in your life your hormones started doing their thing—you know, the music you've already formed a bond with. Why isn't other music as good as that? Right?!

I've got bad (good?) news if you're thinking that kind of nonsense—it's you. Sorry, it is. It's not that there's no good music being made. It's you. You might be getting old. Because I'm here to tell you music is generally good stuff. A song that works usually keeps working. New songs find new people. And they tend to find the people who need them the most. Sometimes I hear new artists and think, "Oh, I wish I could hear what's really going on here." But it's not really for me. I'm not saying I'm being intentionally excluded or that it would necessarily be wrong if I were. Cool trick if you can create something that enforces its own boundaries as it makes its way into the world.

Punk rock set out to police its own borders, but to no avail. People found it, saw themselves in it, and before long you had a CBGB's gift shop at LaGuardia. Along the way it passed through the hands of all sorts of creeps. Neo-Nazis, in particular, found it irresistible. Probably because of the implied intention to segregate and piss off the "right" people. None of that is worth exploring much further than it's already been explored. Agendas are pretty antithetical to music, in my opinion.

Okay, where was I? Correct. I was about to pat myself on the back for not being like that. Not being someone who thinks music is bad because my needs weren't taken into consideration. I'm serious, though. I worked through some stuff to figure that out, and I'm proud of it. And I'm rewarded for my effort to keep an open mind by all of the incredible stuff I get to hear because I went TO it instead of expecting it to come looking for me, hat in hand—"Excuse us, Mr. Tweedy, would you find us more interesting and authentic if we incorporated some electric guitar?"

Not being ridiculous about one's own expectations gives us older folks a chance to appreciate someone like Billie Eilish and her brother, Finneas, for what they truly are: impeccably gifted stylists whose unique talents would have propelled them to stardom in almost any era of modern music. They make hyperreal pop music using digital technology and mic-ing techniques that emphasize the twists and turns of a quiet vocal to the point where a single cracked syllable becomes an arena-sized gesture. (It's possible they invented ASMR pop, although I think my friend Feist might have a stronger claim.)

And yet for all of their modernity, it's easy to picture almost any of their songs being sung leaning on a piano in some tiny jazz club. Which I guess is a way of saying that I did, in fact, find something specific in their music to relate to through the lens of my individual taste. True. But the point is, if you look for music that moves you, you're going to end up finding a way into more music than you might think.

One of the things I've gotten into the habit of doing when I hear a song I love is to pick up my guitar and see if I can learn it. To me it's a way to get one step closer to a song and a songwriter, and I feel privileged to have the ability to access other people's songs by playing them.

What I heard when I played this song to myself was nowhere near as pleasing to my ears as Billie's version. I'm a happy husband and father of two—I'm far away from the world she's living in, and the heartsick circumstances her lyrics are so directly addressing, so it struck me as odd that I could feel them so deeply as my own.

But music is the only language really being spoken here. And when a melody is this profound and beautiful, it makes belief transferable. She and her brother believed it enough for all of us to feel it. There is no greater feat a songwriter can achieve. When a song works this well, we're not only not alone anymore, we are in the presence of greatness.

PORTLAND STORY

HOW AFTER MANY YEARS OF VISITING CITIES AROUND the world, I've developed repetitive patterns and maybe even what would be considered rituals in many of them.

Returning to the exact spots I know I've been to in the past gives me a feeling of grounding that would otherwise get depleted by a nomadic lifestyle. I'm comforted by retracing my steps.

For example—many, many years ago, just before *Being There* came out, I was in Portland, Maine, where Bob Ludwig was mastering our record. One evening I went for a walk on a paved path that runs alongside the narrow-gauge railroad next to the briny water of Casco Bay. Just past a sewage treatment plant and right as the trail began to descend underneath a highway overpass, I came across a makeshift memorial. Some plastic flowers, burned-down candles, a couple of crosses, a teddy bear, and a few xeroxed photos of some kids who appeared to be teenagers. Rain had splotched and warped the smiling faces and names on the pages beyond easy recognition, but "Rest in Peace" remained remarkably clear. Everything else—the flowers, the candles, the teddy bear—all still radiated with a fresh vitality. This had just happened.

Back in my hotel room later that evening, I researched to the best of my ability and the midnineties internet's capability what might have happened to these kids. Morbid curiosity? Maybe. But I felt compelled nonetheless.

I learned that four were killed. I learned their names. Make of their automobile. Early morning. Single-car crash. Prom.

Nearly every visit to Portland since, I've made the trek out to visit the same spot.

The first time after my first encounter, the memorial had been formalized with a stone bench and a plaque with three names. Each followed by the familiar year-to-year span that indicates a lifetime. One life that lasted sixteen years. And two that had managed an extra year. In the weeds nearby, some of the original plastic flowers were still keeping watch.

Second revisit seemed to have coincided with some anniversary or possibly a birthday. Fresh flowers. New teddy bear.

That was the last time any of my visits have provided physical evidence of any loved ones tending to their memory. Although I'm sure someone somewhere is still thinking about them.

I mean, besides me.

One visit, maybe ten or twelve years ago, was the first time I had trouble locating "the spot." Roadside vegetation had engulfed the stone bench, and it took some kicking around in the weeds and brush to uncover it.

The last few times, nothing. Somehow the bench has disappeared. I've looked carefully at the rocks and debris nearby, hopeful I could find some smaller pieces of a former bench that had been broken down by weather or perhaps vandalized. It's gone.

But it's not. I still think about it. And them. I even remember the fourth name that had been left off the plaque.

So why share such a sad and brutal tale of mortality and how nearby oblivion looms?

Because I'm still here. And I can. And they can't tell you. They didn't get the chance.

I love them.

And I love seeing where I've been and being reminded I'm still here.

47

WHO LOVES THE SUN

IN THE EARLY 2000S, LOOSE FUR, A BAND JIM O'ROURKE, Glenn Kotche, and I had started mostly to document the music that seemed to spontaneously compose itself whenever the three of us were in the same room at the same time, played a couple of shows in New York. They ended up being the only real shows we ever played. And one of the nights was also the only time I'm aware of that I performed for Lou Reed.

Thankfully, I wasn't apprised of his presence until after the show. Knowing he was out there would have wrecked me like almost no one else could have. So I'm grateful to whoever made the call to keep it under wraps. It was a big deal to me. The biggest deal you can imagine. To put it in perspective, imagine someone coming up to you after a Little League baseball game and saying, "Hey, guess what? Babe Ruth was in the stands," or after a grade school performance of *Bye Bye Birdie*, maybe someone tells you, "Shakespeare was here! I saw him tapping his foot."

So Lou Reed was there, and for a brief moment at least, he was aware of my existence. Which is ridiculous to care about. But I do, so sue me. We never met and I'm pretty okay with that, considering how awful his reputation was when it came to making people feel like shit. I have met his wife, Laurie Anderson, a few times, and she is the absolute best. So warm and inviting. And that makes me think Lou couldn't have been all that bad.

Still, just knowing he was at a show I played feels complete to me, and it also sidesteps the likelihood he might have called me a schmuck or made me cry with a withering stare. It's hard to explain how one grumpy dude could wield so much perceived power—make so many people unsure of their own worth and fear his judgment. I think it has something to do with this: To a lot of us, Lou Reed represents the triumph of form over beauty, ideas over sentiment, honesty over bullshit, vision over acceptance. He flipped off all of the phonies for us. And he made it clear who the phonies were, and underlined how little technical perfection mattered if all you were going to do with it was pander to the powers that be.

He possessed the rawest form of raw talent—the ability to shape the world around him to meet his own ends. It's a terrifying power. Of course, when you dig through history there are lots of Lou Reeds. They're the ones who remind people that the world doesn't have to be this way. And even more important, they're the ones who remind every misfit alive that fitting in isn't all it's cracked up to be, so you might as well step out into the light.

Which brings us back to why it's such a daunting prospect to be deemed "less than" and humiliated by the guy who gave you permission to be yourself in the first place. How agonizing would it be to have Lou Reed say, in effect, "No, not you! Everyone else. Junkies, deviants, misanthropes, Metallica . . . Yes! You? No. You suck!"

So, "Who Loves the Sun"? Apparently "not everyone," as the song says. Which, taken purely at face value, feels like a high five to this beach skeptic. Of course, it means much more than that. Like a sizable majority of the VU catalog, this song asks the question, "Am I not fitting in?" and before anyone can answer, we get the rhetorical follow-up, "So what!?"

You see the word "misanthrope" get used a lot in relation to the overall impression Lou Reed made on the world. But I think there was an incredible positivity to the Velvet Underground that goes against all the sordid narratives of decadence and societal decay. I mean, that's pretty obvious by now, right? What entered in as deviance and subversiveness ended up being paid out in acceptance and consolation for a fuck-ton of people. Before the internet, this was how people found each other and formed families without blood ties.

That, in my opinion, was the great revolutionary leap this band made. It was the opening of the doors of inclusion to so many weirdos like me. You know, alienated but not all that weird really. And even bigger, more legit weirdos. It wasn't the championing of drugs or sexual transgression. Not the darkness. It didn't speak solely to the participants of subterranean pursuits. No. I look at it more in a sheep-in-wolf's-clothing kind of way—"Yes, we are wearing dark clothes. We are very scary. Let's look at the seamy underbelly of life together, shall we?" but the "TOGETHER" part ended up being the subtle affirming subtext most people heard—"Oh, you'd like that? Well, make yourself right at home."

What their records did was offer a legitimate and believable ray of sunlight to those who would never stomach being pandered to with talk of togetherness and love. For people burdened by their own minds who stumbled upon these records (at any point, from the day they were released to yesterday), life got a tiny bit easier. The Velvet Underground (and let's face it, Andy Warhol) plowed the fields with a clear strategy for living. Accept your friends. Make some art with your friends. Support them even when they sort of suck sometimes. There. You have a family. Now go forth and proliferate.

48

I'M INTO SOMETHING GOOD

HAS THERE EVER BEEN A MORE EFFERVESCENT SONG than this Carole King–penned Herman's Hermits hit? I don't think so. It's like the opposite of the blues. What would that be color-wise? Yellow? As in: "Hey, man, what are you smiling about?"—"Who, me? Dunno, I guess I've just got the yellows."

Point is, it's delightful and I love it. And what makes me love it even more is the fact that it's my wife Susie's favorite song from her childhood. Or at least it was until I ruined it for her. Back before we were married, when I first learned of her deep affection for all things Peter Noone (Herman) and "I'm into Something Good" specifically, I set out to impress her by learning it on guitar so I could sing it for her and make her swoon.

Problem is, I learned it wrong. It went like this: One day we're sitting around just hanging out and I go, "Hey, Susie, check it out!" and I start singing, "Woke up this morning feeling fine . . ." Instantly, Susie is up off the couch singing along and doing some sort of era-specific *Hullabaloo* dance. I'm thinking to myself, "I now know the secret to unearthing unlimited joy at any moment." I felt like how one of those snake charmers must feel the first time they get a cobra to stand up in a basket and do a jig with their flute. Don't tell Susie I compared her to a cobra.

Okay. Things were going great. Then I realized I only really learned the first part of the song. So I stretched out the last "Something tells me I'm into something gooooooood" before I got to the cliff's edge of unknown chords and lyrics and stopped. How did Susie respond, you ask? "Crestfallen" is a word that comes to mind. But that doesn't really convey the implicit anger I was sensing. Susie stopped dancing and moaned, "What gives?!?" like the preteen girl she had just morphed into.

Now, instead of cutting my losses and telling her I'd learn the rest later, I decided to press on. "How hard could it be?" I thought, knowing vaguely where the song was headed from memory. As I stumbled through wrong chords and wrong lyrics, Susie looked on, shaking her head like a rabbi aghast at a bar mitzvah's mangling of their haftarah. Which isn't far off for her, really. What I was doing was sacrilegious. I was desecrating a sacred text.

So here's where things get weird. I have seriously tried, repeatedly, to learn this song correctly, to redeem myself in the eyes of the love of my life, but it eludes me. There's something about how it all goes together that doesn't make sense to me. Or maybe I've just been conditioned to self-sabotage whenever I get close to the scene of the crime—let's call it "the bridge."

Luckily, my failure to nail this one song down has become a running family joke. The joke being that I start singing the song, Susie gets excited, I fuck it up, and Susie gets comically furious.

At least I think it's a joke. In a way it's fitting. That song belongs to her and whatever imaginary (don't tell her I called it imaginary) relationship she has with Herman or Peter Noone (or Peter No One, as I like to call him). I could never compete with the purity of a pop music fantasy. And why bother, when we have the real thing?

HEART OF GLASS

FINDING OUT MY BROTHER WAS HAVING SERIOUS HEART problems from my sister on the phone backstage at an outdoor venue in Montana.

As I'm hanging up, I see a car slow down and stop on a service road parallel to the security fencing. A man gets out and starts running toward me, shouting my name.

Against my normal instinct to hide, I wait for him at the fence. He says he wants to give me something.

Still shaken up from the news of my brother's grim situation, I wait as he runs back to his car to retrieve the item he wants me to have.

Before he unveils my gift, I'm told a bit about his personal history and how my music fits into his own salvation. Short story: Did a lot of drugs. Ended up in jail. Got clean (with the help of *Sky Blue Sky*, he says). Learned the art of glassblowing in prison and now teaches glassblowing to prisoners. As he talks, I begin to really feel connected to the guy. Can't explain it other than maybe family was already on my mind. Whatever it is, this man and his story start feeling like they belong to some shared family history. My mother collected glass paperweights when she was alive, and his mention of glassblowing surely led my mind to her memory.

I start picturing the color red as he talks on. My mother's favorite color. I picture the countless ruby-red glass eggs, globes, and obelisks that occupied entire shelves of her collection. Before he stops talking I know what he's going to give me. I can see it clearly in my mind's eye.

I'm not particularly prone to this type of thing. I believe in a lot, but when things get outright magical, I resist. But here's the thing—I love that we can have these moments that might be better explained by the reality that coincidences occur and the world would be much weirder if nothing ever lined up in lovely serendipitous circles and parallels—moments that nonetheless feel profound, meaningful, and outside of normal explanation. I think it's important we remain open to these moments. Recognizing that we sometimes need things to NOT just make sense. We're desperately in need of experiences that blow our minds with wonder and humble us back into our place in the scary beautiful cosmic mystery we're all blindly swimming around in.

He hands me the gift he brought with him to the show in the hopes that we'd meet.

Slowly unwrapping a heart-sized, crimson, hand-blown glass paperweight.

My dead mother's heart. My sick brother's heart. My sister's heart. My heart.

I wept.

It's on my amp every night.

49

I'M BEGINNING
TO SEE THE LIGHT

I never cared much for moonlit skies
I never winked back at fireflies
But now that the stars are in your eyes
I'm beginning to see the light

I learned this Duke Ellington, Johnny Hodges, Harry James, and Don George–penned song from a cheap compilation CD of early Ellington tracks.

There's a more famous version, sung by Ella Fitzgerald, but Joya Sherrill is the vocalist on this version, the one that stole my heart. The starry-eyed feeling of falling in love in spite of one's defenses—the melting away of a jaded exterior—so clearly stated with simple visual metaphors and similes. It's madly romantic. Too-good-to-be-true lyricism that makes even the faintest smile audible. No matter who's singing.

Which is just one of the reasons I started singing it to

Spencer and Sammy at bedtime. A great song works even when repurposed for familial love. And I've never found a song that better expressed the feeling of wonder I had at discovering the deep abiding love I have for my children. Nothing prepared me for that. And this song helped me make sense of it a little bit. Sure, it's a song to be sung lover to lover. But that never bothered me. Even when the lyrics hit the romance side a little too square on the head, it really doesn't matter when you're singing to a couple of little humans who can light even the darkest days.

50

I'LL TAKE YOU THERE

HERE'S SOMETHING THAT ANYONE WHO'S EVER BEEN over to our house knows. At some point in the evening, Susie is going to turn on the incredible 1957 Seeburg jukebox I bought her for her fiftieth birthday and punch B-12, the ceremonial first number of any dance party in the Tweedy household. "I'll Take You There" by the Staple Singers. This began even before we had any relationship with the woman herself.

The actual 45 being loaded onto the spindle belonged to Susie as a kid, way before jukebox life. It's amazing how Mavis Staples and her family were woven into our lives so deeply that when I finally met her, it felt like a reunion. Even stranger, she felt it, too. It just felt like we were family right off the bat. Which I think says a lot more about Mavis and the way she's been able to openly embrace the world around her than it does about us. We're just a couple of people among the millions who have fallen in love with her, and with each other with Mavis by our side. I've gotten close enough to her over the years to watch her welcome other strangers like long-lost kin, so I know there's a little bit of wish casting going on. But we did hit it off enough to make a lot of music together.

One of the first discussions Mavis and I ever had on the phone, when we were still feeling for a way to collaborate, led us to the notion that as far apart as we may seem to the outside world in terms of genre and life experience, what we had in common was far more important—the idea that all anyone is really accomplishing by lifting up their voice in song is to let the world know they're here. Not to show off or brag or put one over on anyone. But because it made us feel better.

And we both understood that any song worth singing could never have begun with our singular voices. We both believed in something much larger than a single voice or song, something we knew from experience. When we had been alone, the songs sung to us unlocked us from our isolation. And allowed us to sing. Our own songs? Maybe. But nothing so important could be or should be believed to be wholly owned by anyone.

Mavis and I wrote a song together to reflect our shared sweet, hopeful understanding of what it actually is that we do when we sing and when others listen to our songs. It has to do with loneliness, and how much of it there is. I'm here. You're here. That's all that can really be said.

It's heartbreaking and simple. Uplifting and difficult. So, we wrote our first song together to acknowledge the core task at hand. "You Are Not Alone." I personally think of this song in an extremely literal sense. I imagine it's because I spent so much time factually alone in my bedroom being comforted by my record collection. So I always picture any type of person you can imagine— headbanger, goth kid, accountant—alone in a room, confronting a faded connection with the world, being told by our song exactly what I most wanted every song to tell me. You. Are. Not. Alone.

It's a wonderful feeling to have a hand on your shoulder. What else is there?

Every time Susie and I dance in our living room to "I'll Take You There," I'm reminded of how sweet it was of Mavis to not remind me that she'd been singing our song way before we wrote it. But then again, she gets it. She knows that it's not something you do once and then you're done. You don't get "there" and stay. Every day, you get up and search for it again. Mavis knows the way. We all do. You just have to sing along.

ACKNOWLEDGMENTS

Even though I believe that I've stated clearly enough throughout this book that my primary objective has not been to provide an overview of songs and songwriters I judge to be of the greatest value to all, I'm still feeling a bit queasy when I think of some of this book's most egregious omissions: Your Neil Youngs . . . your Lana Del Reys . . . your Smokey Robinsons . . . your Kurt Cobains . . . your Arethas . . . your Cohens, and your Yankovics . . . I honestly could go on for at least another one thousand pages.

So with one last plea for forgiveness to the acknowledgment gods and goddesses for all of the unintentionally overlooked beauty and inspiration, I'd like to first bow deeply to all of the artists past, present, and future, who shape not just me but my own songs, and then by extension, anyone kind enough to listen closely when I sing. It's truly a wonder to be a part of something so vast and imposing yet able to fit through the smallest cracks in any human heart. It's the only club I've ever really wanted to belong to. I know there aren't dues or oaths to take or any prerequisites . . . and no one asked me to join. Nonetheless, it is a massive collection of humanity I cherish counting myself among, that dream-bent and magically flawed sub-phylum of musicians known as songwriters. In "Tower of Song," Leonard Cohen claims Hank Williams lives a hundred floors above him. Whenever I hear that lyric, I think about how happy I am to have found a place for myself in that same "Tower" by way of a small sublet room in the unfinished basement.

All I'm saying is—I owe a lot to a lot of people who aren't mentioned. I wish I could tell you all everything about what they all mean to me. But I can't. Plus, that wouldn't leave me enough space to acknowledge you. Which is hopefully the clearest message made by these pages. What we individually bring to a song matters a lot. In the economy of listening, a song is worth whatever WE make of it. So while this book is technically about the songs I'm made of, and what I've made of the songs I've loved (and hated), none of it would make any sense without the faith I have in everyone's ability to absorb and be absorbed by music.

Including yours. So thank you. Good job!

"Don't Think Twice, It's All Right"
Written and recorded by Bob Dylan
From the album *The Freewheelin' Bob Dylan*
    (Columbia, 1963)

"Mull of Kintyre"
Written by Paul McCartney and Denny Laine
Recorded by Wings
From the album *Wings Greatest* (Capitol, 1978)

"Loud, Loud, Loud"
Written by Vangelis Papathanassiou and Costas Ferris
Recorded by Aphrodite's Child
From the album *666* (Vertigo, 1972)

"Both Sides Now"
Written and recorded by Joni Mitchell
From the album *Clouds* (Reprise, 1969)

"Lucky Number"
Written by Lene Lovich and Les Chappell
Recorded by Lene Lovich
From the album *Stateless* (Stiff, 1978)

"Gloria"
Written by Patti Smith and Van Morrison
Recorded by Patti Smith
From the album *Horses* (Arista, 1975)

"As If It Always Happens"
Written and recorded by Slovenly
From the album *Riposte* (SST, 1987)

"Somewhere Over the Rainbow"
Written by E. Y. Harburg and Harold Arlen
Recorded by Judy Garland
From the album *The Wizard of Oz* (Decca, 1940)

"Death or Glory"
Written by Joe Strummer and Mick Jones
Recorded by The Clash
From the album *London Calling* (CBS, 1979)

"My Sharona"
Written by Doug Fieger and Berton Averre
Recorded by The Knack
From the album *Get the Knack* (Capitol, 1979)

"In Germany Before the War"
Written by Randy Newman
Recorded by Randy Newman
From the album *Little Criminals* (Warner Bros., 1977)

"Dancing Queen"
Written by Benny Andersson, Björn Ulvaeus,
   and Stig Anderson
Recorded by ABBA
From the album *Arrival* (Atlantic, 1976)

"The Message"
Written by Edward G. Fletcher, Melle Mel, Clifton
   "Jiggs" Chase, and Sylvia Robinson
Recorded by Grandmaster Flash and the Furious Five
From the album *The Message* (Sugar Hill, 1982)

"Balancing Act"
Written by Peter Prescott
Recorded by Volcano Suns
From the album *The Bright Orange Years*
   (Homestead Records, 1985)

"Frankie Teardrop"
Written by Alan Vega and Martin Rev
Recorded by Suicide
From the album *Suicide* (Red Star, 1977)

"I'm Not in Love"
Written by Graham Gouldman and Eric Stewart
Recorded by 10cc
From the album *The Original Soundtrack* (Mercury, 1975)

"Connection"
Written by Mick Jagger and Keith Richards
Recorded by The Rolling Stones
From the album *Between the Buttons*
    (Decca/ABKCO UK, London/ABKCO US, 1967)

"Forever Paradise"
Written by J. J. O'Neill
Recorded by The Undertones
From the album *Positive Touch* (Harvest, 1981)

"Satan, Your Kingdom Must Come Down"
Recorded by Frank Proffitt
From the album *High Atmosphere: Ballads and
    Banjo Tunes from Virginia and North Carolina*
    (Rounder Records, 1975)

"God Damn Job"
Written by Paul Westerberg
Recorded by The Replacements
From the EP *Stink* (Twin/Tone, 1982)

"Ramblin' Man"
Written by Dickey Betts
Recorded by The Allman Brothers Band
From the album *Brothers and Sisters* (Capricorn, 1973)

"History Lesson—Part II"
Written by Mike Watt
Recorded by Minutemen
From the album *Double Nickels on the Dime* (SST, 1984)

"Little Johnny Jewel"
Written by Tom Verlaine
Recorded by Television
From the album *Marquee Moon* (Bonus Tracks)
    (Elektra, 2003)

"4'33""
Composed by John Cage

"Anchorage"
Written by Michelle Shocked
Recorded by Michelle Shocked
From the album *Short Sharp Shocked* (Mercury, 1988)

"(Sittin' on) The Dock of the Bay"
Written by Steve Cropper and Otis Redding
Recorded by Otis Redding
From the single "(Sittin' on) The Dock of the Bay"
    (Stax Records, 1968)

"You Are My Sunshine"
Performed by The Carter Family
From the album *The Carter Family on Border Radio,*
    vol. 3: 1939 (Arhoolie Records, 1999)

"I Will Always Love You"
Written by Dolly Parton
Recorded by Dolly Parton
From the album *Jolene* (RCA Victor, 1974)

"Wanted Dead or Alive"
Written by Jon Bon Jovi and Richie Sambora
Recorded by Jon Bon Jovi
From the album *Slippery When Wet* (Mercury, 1987)

"Before Tonight"
Written by Joe Adducci
From the album *Notes Campfire* (Moll Tonträger, 1996)

"Shotgun"
Written by Autry DeWalt (Junior Walker)
Recorded by Junior Walker & the All Stars
From the single "Shotgun" (Soul Records, 1965)

"The Weight"
Written by Robbie Robertson
Recorded by The Band
From the album *Music from Big Pink* (Capitol, 1968)

"Will You Love Me Tomorrow"
Written by Gerry Goffin and Carole King
Recorded by The Shirelles
From the album *Tonight's the Night* (Scepter, 1960)

"Free Bird"
Written by Allen Collins and Ronnie Van Zant
Recorded by Lynyrd Skynyrd
From the album *(Pronounced 'Lĕh-'nérd 'Skin-'nérd)*
   (MCA, 1973)

"The Star-Spangled Banner"
Written by Francis Scott Key
   (from his poem "Defence of Fort M'Henry")
Set to the tune of "To Anacreon in Heaven"
   by John Stafford Smith

"Radio Free Europe"
Written by Bill Berry, Peter Buck, Mike Mills,
   and Michael Stipe
Recorded by R.E.M.
From the album *Murmur* (I.R.S., 1983)

"I'm Against It"
Written by Douglas Colvin, John Cummings,
   and Jeff Hyman
Recorded by Ramones
From the album *Road to Ruin* (Sire, 1978)

"Bizcochito"
Written by Rosalía Vila, David Rodríguez,
    and Michael Uzowuru
Recorded by Rosalía
From the album *Motomami* (Columbia, 2022)

"Close My Eyes"
Written by Arthur Russell
Recorded by Arthur Russell
From the album *Love Is Overtaking Me* (Audika, 2008)

"Happy Birthday"

"Love Like a Wire"
Written by Diane Izzo

"I Love You"
Written by Billie Eilish O'Connell and Finneas O'Connell
Recorded by Billie Eilish
From the album *When We All Fall Asleep, Where Do We Go?*
    (Darkroom, 2019)

"Who Loves the Sun"
Written by Lou Reed
Recorded by The Velvet Underground
From the album *Loaded* (Cotillion, 1970)

"I'm into Something Good"
Written by Gerry Goffin and Carole King
Recorded by Herman's Hermits
From the album *Herman's Hermits* (MGM, 1964)

"I'm Beginning to See the Light"
Written by Duke Ellington, Don George, Johnny Hodges,
    and Harry James
Recorded by Duke Ellington and his orchestra, with vocals
    by Joya Sherrill
From the single "I'm Beginning to See the Light"
    (RCA, 1944)

"I'll Take You There"
Written by Al Bell
Recorded by The Staple Singers
From the album *Be Altitude: Respect Yourself* (Stax, 1972)

ABOUT THE AUTHOR

As the founding member and leader of the Grammy Award–winning American rock band Wilco, and before that the cofounder of the alt-country band Uncle Tupelo, **Jeff Tweedy** is one of contemporary music's most accomplished songwriters, musicians, and performers. Jeff has released two solo albums, has written original songs for twelve Wilco albums, and is the author of the *New York Times* bestsellers *Let's Go (So We Can Get Back): A Memoir of Recording and Discording with Wilco, Etc.* and *How to Write One Song*. He lives in Chicago with his family.

MAXnotes

John Steinbeck's

The Grapes of Wrath

Text by
Lee Cusick
(M.A., Northern Arizona University)
Department of English, Speech, and Drama
Fabens High School
Fabens, Texas

Illustrations by
Michael A. Kupka

Research & Education Association

813.09
STEINBECK, J
CUSICK, L

MAXnotes™ for
THE GRAPES OF WRATH

Printed in the United States of America

Library of Congress Catalog Card Number 94-65966

International Standard Book Number 0-87891-947-3

MAXnotes™ is a trademark of
Research & Education Association, Piscataway, New Jersey 08854

What **MAXnotes**™ *Will Do for You*

This book is intended to help you absorb the essential contents and features of John Steinbeck's *The Grapes of Wrath* and to help you gain a thorough understanding of the work. The book has been designed to do this more quickly and effectively than any other study guide.

For best results, this **MAXnotes** book should be used as a companion to the actual work, not instead of it. The interaction between the two will greatly benefit you.

To help you in your studies, this book presents the most up-to-date interpretations of every section of the actual work, followed by questions and fully explained answers that will enable you to analyze the material critically. The questions also will help you to test your understanding of the work and will prepare you for discussions and exams.

Meaningful illustrations are included to further enhance your understanding and enjoyment of the literary work. The illustrations are designed to place you into the mood and spirit of the work's settings.

The **MAXnotes** also include summaries, character lists, explanations of plot, and chapter-by-chapter analyses. A biography of the author and discussion of the work's historical context will help you put this literary piece into the proper perspective of what is taking place.

The use of this study guide will save you the hours of preparation time that would ordinarily be required to arrive at a complete grasp of this work of literature. You will be well-prepared for classroom discussions, homework, and exams. The guidelines that are included for writing papers and reports on various topics will prepare you for any added work which may be assigned.

The **MAXnotes** will take your grades "to the max."

Dr. Max Fogiel
Program Director

Contents

> **Each unit includes List of Characters,**
> **Summary, Analysis, Study Questions and**
> **Answers, and Suggested Essay Topics.**

SECTION ONE

Introduction

The Life and Work of John Steinbeck

John Steinbeck was born on February 27, 1902, in Salinas, California. In the course of his life he was a common laborer, store clerk, ranch hand, surveyor, world traveler, journalist, short story writer, essayist, and playwright, as well as the author of 18 novels. His novels about the common people and the troubles that beset them earned him his reputation as one of America's greatest writers.

He attended Stanford University sporadically between 1919 and 1925, but earned very few credits in his major field, marine biology, often taking one term off to work and earn enough to pay for the next. During this period he began writing fiction in the form of short stories. No doubt he was inspired to be a writer at an early age by having many famous pieces of literature read to him by his mother, a former school teacher.

A short attempt at freelance writing in New York City in 1925 proved futile. Returning to California proved to be his salvation, and most of his writings used places and subjects from this area. He had grown up in the Salinas Valley, worked on farms and ranches while attending Stanford, and later took much of the material used in the creation of several of his novels from his experiences and surroundings.

Steinbeck never lost his desire to write and finally achieved popularity and success with his novel *Tortilla Flat* in 1935. With the publication of his novel *Of Mice and Men,* in 1937, he became a national figure. Perhaps his most popular and greatest work, however, was *The Grapes of Wrath.* Published in 1939, it reached the top of the best-seller list within two months, and Steinbeck was awarded the Pulitzer Prize for it in 1940. It has been hailed as a masterpiece and a landmark in American literature. However, following his great success with this novel, his reputation declined with the appearance of lesser works such as *The Winter of Our Discontent.*

Steinbeck seemed to lose interest in writing fiction in the early 1960s, and in his last years he was more active as a traveler and journalist and writer of nonfiction. Two of the notable examples of this phase of his life were *Travels with Charley in Search of America* and *America and Americans.*

Steinbeck wrote about ordinary people doing battle against dehumanizing social forces or struggling against their own inhumane tendencies and trying to forge lives of meaning and worth. In his writing, he did not attempt to entertain but rather to present the raw and bitter moments of the true life situations he observed around him, often living and working with people who later served as the models for his characters. He actually traveled the road from Oklahoma to California along with "Dust Bowl" migrants as research for *The Grapes of Wrath.*

Steinbeck was awarded the Nobel Prize for Literature in 1962, in recognition of the entire body of his work. He died on December 20, 1968 in New York City.

Historical Background

When Steinbeck wrote *The Grapes of Wrath*, the United States was suffering through a severe economic depression. Everywhere people lost their savings, homes, and means of earning a living. Especially hard hit were the farming areas of the Midwest. Poor farming practices had depleted the soil, and it became less capable of supporting the individual families who farmed their small sections of it. Also, the markets and prices for the crops declined. Agriculture markedly changed in the area as a result. Small farms were consolidated into larger, and more profitable units. Tractors, other machines, and day laborers replaced mules and family labor. Independent farm life, which had developed the area and dominated it during the 1800s, dwindled. In the mid-1930s there were severe droughts and erosion of the dry soil by strong winds. This created a "Dust Bowl" in the states of Oklahoma, Texas, Kansas, and Colorado. The small farmers, now tenants and sharecroppers, were uprooted from the homes and farms which had belonged to their families for many years. By the tens of thousands these victims of depression, drought, and dust headed west to seek a better life in the fertile fields of California. They found themselves as much victims there. Work was scarce, wages were low, and they were resented, resisted, and repressed by the residents. Their attempts to better their lives were branded as Communism, a system much disliked and feared by many Americans of the time.

Reaction to *The Grapes of Wrath* was immediate, and ran to extremes of praise and condemnation. One noted critic said the book might do for its time what *Uncle Tom's Cabin* did for its, because it so strongly exposed social injustice and called for social redress; but many people denounced it as Communist propaganda. People in California and Oklahoma charged it was full of exaggerated lies about the conditions and treatment of the migrants in their respective states. In California, one writer refuted point-by-point what he labeled the book's inaccuracies. A Congressman from Oklahoma denounced it, on behalf of the people of his state, on the floor of the House of Representatives as "a dirty, lying, filthy manuscript-a lie, a damnable lie, a black, infernal creation of a twisted, distorted mind."

Copies of the book were symbolically burned in a town in Illinois by order of the Library Board, even as the librarian noted that the waiting list for it was longer than for any other book in history. The burning order came in the same week the book had its largest sales in seven months. Indeed, the general public embraced *The Grapes of Wrath*. It became a best-seller shortly after publication and has been in print and widely read continuously since that time. The story was also made into a successful major motion picture starring Henry Fonda. A crowning accolade for the novel was the award of the 1940 Pulitzer Prize for fiction to Steinbeck.

Master List of Characters

Tom Joad—*A farmer's son. He has just been paroled from prison and joins his family for a trip to California when he learns they have lost their farm.*

Pa Joad—*Called "Old Tom." A dispossessed tenant farmer. He hopes to find farm work in California.*

Ma Joad—*Tom's mother, the mainstay of the family. Her main goals are to keep the family strong, fed, and together.*

Grampa and Granma Joad—*Pa Joad's elderly parents. They settled the 40-acre farm in Oklahoma from which the family is now uprooted.*

Noah Joad—*Tom's quiet and slow-witted older brother.*

Al Joad—*Pa and Ma's third son, a 16-year-old whose foremost interests are girls and cars.*

Ruthie and Winfield Joad—*At 12 and 10 years of age respectively, they are the youngest daughter and son in the Joad family.*

Rose of Sharon—*Tom's young, newly married sister who is expecting a child, and yearns for a good home for it.*

Connie—*Rose of Sharon's equally young and ambitious husband.*

Uncle John—*Pa's withdrawn and brooding brother.*

Jim Casy—*A friend of the family and former preacher who joins with the Joads for the trip to California.*

Muley Graves—*A neighbor of the Joad's who has also been dispossessed but hides and lives like an animal on his land because he cannot bring himself to leave it.*

Ivy and Sarah Wilson—*A migrant couple who join the Joads and travel with them after the Joads give them help on the road to California.*

Jim Rawley—*The manager of a clean and orderly camp provided by the government to better the migrants' living conditions.*

Ezra Huston—*The chairman of the central committee by means of which the migrants govern themselves in the camp.*

Mr. and Mrs. Wainwright—*A couple who share a boxcar home near a cotton field with the Joads.*

Aggie Wainwright—*The Wainwrights' daughter who becomes engaged to Al Joad.*

Summary of the Novel

Tom Joad, a prison parolee, meets Jim Casy, a preacher who has given up his calling. They go to Tom's home looking for his family, but the Joad farm and all those around it are deserted. They are told the Joads are living with Tom's Uncle John. Arriving at Uncle John's house, they learn the family has lost their farm and are making preparations to sell their belongings and move to California in search of promised work.

With Casy accompanying them, the Joads encounter many hardships on the road west, and the family crumbles. Grampa dies the first night he is separated from his beloved land. Granma dies while they are crossing the Arizona desert. Noah and Connie give up and leave the family. The further west they go, the more resistant and unfriendly the people are.

In California the family goes from camp to camp in a futile search for work and their living conditions worsen. Jim Casy organizes a strike against the unfair low wages being paid and is killed. Tom kills Jim's murderer and goes into hiding. He leaves the family to continue Casy's work. The Joads move to a cottonfield where the pay is better.

Rose of Sharon delivers a stillborn baby during a fearful storm. The family has to abandon their boxcar home to escape the resultant flood. Taking refuge in a hillside barn, they discover a young boy and his near-dead, starving father who is saved when Rose feeds him from her milk-filled breasts.

Estimated Reading Time

The average person should be able to read the entire novel in a total of approximately 12 to 18 hours.

It is suggested that the reading of the novel be divided into the three blocks indicated. These three blocks divide the story into what happens in Oklahoma, on the journey west, and after the migrants arrive in California.

If desired, the reading can be further broken down into the six sub-units listed. In this study guide, study questions and suggested essay topics follow the summary and discussion of each of the six sub-units.

BLOCK ONE:	LEAVING OKLAHOMA	Reading Time: 4–6 hrs.
Unit I	Chapters 1–6	2–3 hrs
Unit II	Chapters 7–11	2–3 hrs
BLOCK TWO:	THE JOURNEY WEST	Reading Time: 4–6 hrs
Unit III	Chapters 12–16	2–3 hrs
Unit IV	Chapters 17–21	2–3 hrs
BLOCK THREE:	LIFE IN CALIFORNIA	Reading Time: 4–6 hrs
Unit V	Chapters 22–26	3–4 hrs
Unit VI	Chapters 27–30	1–2 hrs

Unit I

Chapters 1–6

New Characters:

Tom Joad: *the protagonist, an Oklahoma tenant farmer's son*

Jim Casy: *a former preacher who now questions traditional beliefs as he observes human behavior*

Muley Graves: *a farmer reduced to homeless poverty when he loses his family's land through foreclosure*

Summary

Chapter 1

When the last of light rains ended in early May, the land began to dry up. Weeds changed their color to protect themselves from the harsh sun and the corn faded and dried up. The few drops of rain that fell in June gave no help. Animal hooves and vehicle wheels broke the dry dirt crust and formed dust. Winds drove the dust until it mixed with the air and the sky was dark. When the winds subsided, the dust settled and covered the earth like a blanket. Farm men stood silently and looked at the ruined corn blown down by the wind and covered by the dust. Their women watched the

silent men, and when they saw anger in the men's faces they knew there was still hope as long as the dust did not break the spirit of the men.

Chapter 2

A man dressed in new, but cheap, clothes sees a large truck parked at a roadside cafe. Despite the "No Riders" sign on the truck he asks the driver for a ride. He points out that some drivers are "good guys" even if their bosses make them carry the sign. The driver lets him into the truck, around the corner out of sight of the cafe. The hitchhiker says his name is Tom Joad, and having been away from home for four years, is now returning to his father's 40-acre farm. The driver expresses surprise that someone with only 40 acres has not

been driven out yet. The driver is obviously suspicious of Tom
and talks about studying fingerprints. Tom tells the driver
he has just spent four years of a seven-year sentence for
manslaughter in the state prison and been paroled for good
behavior. He leaves the truck at the road leading to the Joad
farm.

Chapter 3

A land turtle, after a long and difficult climb, finally
reached the highway surface and started slowly across. One
vehicle swerved to miss it, but the driver of a second vehicle
swerved to hit it. The turtle was thrown off the highway and
landed on its back. After struggling for some time the turtle
righted itself and slowly resumed its journey.

Chapter 4

Tom notices the thickness of the dust. He picks up a land
turtle he sees, intending to give it to one of the young children in his family. As he walks toward the farm he meets a
man who recognizes him. This is Jim Casy, the preacher who
baptized Tom and knew Old Tom Joad, his father. He explains
he no longer preaches because he became worried about his
having sexual relations with girls who came to his religious
meetings. Feeling it was not right, he went off to think about
it. He says he now realizes "there ain't no sin and there ain't
no virtues," and that the actions of people are more important than abstract religious concepts.

Tom starts to leave and Casy asks how Old Tom is. Tom
says he does not know because he has been gone for four
years and has not heard from the family. He tells Casy about
having killed a man who stuck a knife in him by hitting the
man with a shovel and about being in prison for the four
years. When Casy asks him his feelings about the killing, Tom
says he had to defend himself and is not ashamed of his ac-

tions. Casy asks about prison life and Tom tells him simply that the prisoners ate regularly and bathed daily. He tells of a man who committed a crime to get sent back to prison because he was hungry.

Casy asks if he can go with him and speak with Old Tom. Tom says he is welcome to do so. As they approach the Joad house, they realize that no one is home and something is wrong.

Chapter 5

The owners of the land, hating what they had to do, came to the tenant families in anger or in grief. Blaming the banks' demand for profit on their money, they explained the tenant farming system wouldn't work anymore. The only way the land could be profitable was to farm larger consolidated sections of it with machines. The tenants knew they couldn't feed their families adequately from their small farms, but

they had no place to go. They had been on the land since it
was settled by their grandparents. Mortgages were fore-
closed, the farms were consolidated, and the tenants had to
leave. Then a tractor hired by a bank or corporation plowed
the fields in long straight lines, knocking down houses or
barns that stood in the way of any such straight line.

When a tractor operator told one tenant he would have
to knock the tenant's house down, the farmer recognized him
as a farm boy named Davis and asked why he was doing this
to his own kind of people. The operator said his own family
was without food and necessary clothing, and he was doing
it because the pay was good. When the farmer threatened to
shoot him, the boy said it would do no good; another tractor
driver would be pushing the house down even before the
farmer was surely hanged for shooting him.

Chapter 6

Tom and Jim approach the Joad house and see that one
corner has been knocked in and the house is pushed out of
shape. Noticing the well is dry and the barn is empty, Tom is
aware something is wrong. He realizes there are no neighbors left when he sees a cat prowling around and nothing is
disturbed. He knows that if only the Joads have moved, the
neighbors would have come and taken the lumber from the
house as well as other things. He releases the turtle he was
bringing for the children. It immediately heads ploddingly
toward the southwest.

Tom and Jim see a dust-covered figure coming down the
road. When Tom recognizes the person as Muley Graves, they
call to him. He is frightened but comes over and recognizes
Tom. He tells Tom that Old Tom is very worried about leaving and being unable to let Tom know about it because he is
such a poor letter writer. Muley gives a long explanation
about what has happened to the farms. Tom finally gets him

to tell where the Joads are. Muley says they have moved to the house of Tom's Uncle John and have been chopping cotton to earn enough money to buy a car in which to go to California.

Muley tells them he has been pushed off his farm and his family has gone to California, but that he could not bring himself to leave his father's land, so he has been hiding on it. He tells them a large company bought up the land and replaced the tenants with tractors and day laborers as they only way to make a profit from the land.

Tom has become hungry and asks Muley about eating. Muley is living off the land and has two rabbits he trapped. He shares these with Tom and Jim, saying there is no choice when one person has food and another doesn't. As headlights approach, Muley says they must hide or be in trouble for trespassing. Tom doesn't want to hide on his own father's land, but is reminded that he is on parole and can't afford trouble.

Tom refuses to sleep in a cave Muley shows him, saying he prefers the open night air.

Analysis

In this unit we are introduced to the format Steinbeck chooses to tell two stories; the larger story of the mass migration of refugees from the southwestern "Dust Bowl" toward the promise of a better life, and the more personal story of the Joads, one family that makes the journey. The story of the Joads is a traditional fictional narrative, while the larger story is told in a variety of styles in intercalary chapters which give background to, and often a parallel to or preview of, what happens to the Joads.

Chapters 1, 3, and 5 are such intercalary chapters. They also establish the story's conflict between man and his physical and social environments. The first describes the forces which created the "Dust Bowl" and the troubles of the farm families there. Chapter 3 is an allegory in which a land turtle symbolizes the common man laboring and struggling to make his way in the world beset by natural and social forces. While Chapter 1 deals with the forces of nature affecting the Joads, Chapter 5 is concerned with the economic and social forces that push them off their land.

It will be through the narrative of the struggles of the Joads that central themes such as social injustice and the family as a source of strength will emerge. Indeed, as the plot unfolds we will see, paralleling the journey west, the movement from one strong family through the strength of a group or family of families to the belief in the unity of the entire family of mankind giving the strength to overcome social injustice.

There is another theme which appears in many scenes in the novel and is later expressly stated by Ma Joad: that when a poor person wants something, he had best go for help to one of his own kind. Here in Unit I this theme is introduced by Tom getting the ride from the truck driver and Muley Graves sharing his meager food. The truck driver is pictured as one of the "good guys" who will help those in need as opposed to the "rich bastards" who are out to destroy the poor. Muley feels there is no choice but to share what little he has with those even less fortunate.

The major theme that what people actually do is more important than abstract concepts about behavior is introduced with the character of Jim Casy. He has renounced his preaching of religious principles because of his own actions, which he saw as sinful according to religious teachings. After a long, lonely, and laborious meditation he has decided that there is no sin or virtue, just what people do.

Thus, Ma and the Joads are not pictured as abstract concepts but as real people, living human beings struggling to survive in a harsh society. Casy also expresses the idea of the unity of mankind in one "oversoul" of which each person is a part. Casy, in contrast to the somewhat self-centered Tom Joad we meet in this unit, is trying to formulate something that will help all mankind. As we will later see, meeting Casy is pivotal to Tom's eventual development. For now it represents the solitary Tom joining forces with another person on his personal journey toward membership in the larger community of mankind.

Chapter 6 initiates the action on Tom's personal journey. Here he wants only to go home to his old life but finds his home destroyed, and he is forced to hide to avoid being arrested for trespassing on the land which had belonged to his father. Though angry at this, he is made to realize his actions and natural instincts will be restricted in the future because of his parole. As his journey progresses, he will become more resentful of his inability to fight back against oppressive conditions he and his family encounter.

Study Questions

1. What signs were the farm women and children watching the men for?

2. Why is the truck driver who gives Tom a ride nameless?

3. Why does the truck driver break the "No Riders" rule of his company?

4. How does the land turtle foreshadow events in the story?

5. What reason does Jim Casy give for no longer preaching?

6. How did the bankers' agents explain foreclosing on mortgages and driving the farmers off of their land?

7. What reason does Muley Graves give for sharing his rabbits?

8. What does the presence of the cat and the condition of the Joad house tell Tom?

9. Why does the author have Tom tell about keeping to himself and not causing trouble in prison?

10. What is the motive for farmers such as Joe Davis' son taking jobs bulldozing other farmers' homes?

Answers

1. The women looked for signs that they had not given up, defeated by the conflict with nature, or that the men still had the spirit to go on. The women could be strong only as long as the men had hope, and the children were aware of this.

2. He is unimportant as an individual character, yet his symbolic representation of the struggle of one class against another is important.

3. He is lonely and wants someone to talk to, and he greatly resents the company policy.

4. The turtle plods along on its way with purpose and tenacity despite encountering many difficulties and setbacks, as will the Joads and the other migrants.

5. He began to consider his own behavior to be sinful while he was preaching against sin. After much meditation he concluded there was no sin or virtue, only what people did, upon which no judgment should be placed.

6. They said the banks needed profits to survive and since the small farms were not providing enough profits they had to be consolidated into larger units.

7. He says there is no choice but to share when one person has food and another person doesn't.

8. Tom realized that all the neighbors were gone too. If only the Joads had left, those remaining would have taken the lumber from the house, and the cat would be better fed.

9. He is establishing Tom as a person primarily concerned with only himself and his own well-being.

10. They are as much the victims of the depression and the drought as the other farmers and have accepted the work to help their families to survive.

Suggested Essay Topics

1. Compare and contrast the characters of Jim Casy and Tom Joad as revealed in their first conversations.

2. Explain the three-fold symbolism of giving the name Muley Graves to the dispossessed farmer.

SECTION THREE

Unit II
Chapters 7–11

New Characters:

Pa Joad: *one of many dispossessed "Dust Bowl" farmers who dream of a better life in California*

Ma Joad: *his strong wife who is devoted to preserving her family*

Grampa Joad: *the elderly, senile patriarch of the family*

Granma Joad: *his wife who is a religious fanatic*

Noah Joad: *the eldest son who moves slowly and says little*

Al Joad: *the Joad's teenage son who is good at working on cars*

Uncle John: *Pa Joad's brother, a widower*

Ruthie and Winfield Joad: *Pa and Ma's youngest children*

Rose of Sharon: *the Joad's married and pregnant daughter*

Connie: *Rose of Sharon's husband*

Summary

Chapter 7

Because there was more profit and demand for used cars and trucks, salesmen were selling them to the dispossessed tenants as quickly as possible. The tenants knew little about cars and the salesmen were able to cheat them on price, interest rates, and quality. They disguised the poor condition of the vehicles in many ways and ignored complaints. They knew the tenants would be driving the vehicles away from the area anyway, so they would get no complaints.

Chapter 8

Muley wakes Tom and Casy before dawn and says he is leaving. Tom and Casy start walking to Uncle John's house. On the way Tom tells Casy that Uncle John has been rather strange and withdrawn since his wife's death, which occurred when he ignored her complaints of pain in the night.

As they near the house, Tom sees furniture stacked out in the yard and realizes the family is about to leave. Pa Joad is working on the car and doesn't recognize Tom at first.

When he does, he wants to know if Tom has broken out of prison. Tom tells Pa about being paroled.

Pa says they are about to leave for California and were going to send Tom a letter because Ma was afraid she would never see Tom again. He takes them into the house for breakfast where Ma, busy cooking, pays no attention to Tom or Casy. When she recognizes Tom, she too is concerned that he has broken out of prison. Assured that he has not, she welcomes him warmly and sends Pa to get Grampa and Granma.

She then asks Tom if prison made him mad. She had known "Pretty Boy" Floyd and prison made him "mean mad," but Tom assures her he is all right. Grampa and Granma race each other from the barn to the house. Noah follows slowly, as he does everything. Grampa and Granma are happy to see Tom. They tell him he should have killed the man but should not have gone to jail for doing it.

At breakfast, Granma insists that Casy, the preacher, say grace. He explains he is not a preacher anymore, but she insists on a prayer. Casy gives a long, rambling recitation of how he went out alone and got to thinking "how we was holy when we was one thing, and mankin' was holy when it was one thing."

Pa shows Tom the car that 16-year-old Al, who learned about machinery on a job he had, helped them buy to make the trip. He says Al is not there because he has been "tom-cattin' hisself to death" for some time. He also tells Tom that Ruthie and Winfield, the two youngest children, have gone with Uncle John to sell some household equipment. Then Al appears and is glad to see Tom, whom he admires and tries to emulate.

Chapter 9

The tenant farmers sorted their possessions to find

things to sell. They had to sell to get money for the trip and because there was no room on the trucks to take much with them. Buyers pretended they weren't interested in buying the things at any price, and the tenants had to sell their farm tools and household furnishings for next to nothing. Discouraged, they went home to tell the women how little they got. The women went through their personal keepsakes to see which of them also had to be disposed of. There was no room on the trucks for items of sentimental value either.

Chapter 10

Ma and Tom have a talk. Ma wonders if California will be as nice as the handbill describing the need for workers there promises. She says she has less faith than she had. Tom reflects that the only way he endured prison life was to live day by day and not think about the future. He says he has heard that the farm workers are poorly paid, housed, and fed, but Ma still has some confidence in what the handbill says. Following this, Grampa rambles on at length about all the delicious grapes he will eat in California.

Jim Casy asks if he can go along with the Joads. Ma says she is sure he is welcome to, but the men of the family will have to decide. Casy says he will preach no more but just wants to be with people. He says being with people is holy in itself.

Pa is "angry and sad" because he only got 18 dollars for the family's possessions when the buyer pretended he didn't want them. Confused, Pa took what he could get although he knew Ma would be disappointed.

During a family council that evening, Al points out the good features of the car he chose and Tom asks about taking Casy along. Pa questions whether there is enough room and food for one more, but Ma reminds him they have never turned anyone down and having only one more won't make

that much difference. They decide to include Casy and have him join the council to help discuss other matters. They decide to slaughter two pigs to eat on the journey and to work all night so they can set off early the next morning. Despite Ma's protest that it is her job, Casy says he will salt down the pig meat because there is too much work to be done to break it down into "men's work and women's work." So Ma goes through her private possessions, selects a very few, and burns the rest.

Muley Graves comes by to say goodbye and have the Joads tell his family he is all right. The Joads offer to take him

with them but as much as he would like to, he just cannot leave the land he knows. Grampa says he is not going either; that he will live like Muley and stay "right where I b'long." The family decides they can't leave Grampa behind, but if they force him to go he will hurt himself. They give him a large dose of sleeping medicine and load him into the truck in a sound, drugged sleep and depart. They give Muley the chickens they still have left.

Chapter 11

The houses were vacant, and without people the land was vacant. The people who had tended the land were replaced by lifeless machinery and artificial fertilizers. The men who now plowed and fertilized were strangers with no understanding of the relation of men to the land. Empty, the houses ceased to be houses. They were overrun by animals and weeds and were soon torn apart by the severe elements of nature.

Analysis

The intercalary chapters in this unit again serve to point out that the plight of the Joads is not unique to them alone but affects a whole society. They set the stage on which the drama of the Joads is played out and foreshadow events in the narrative. Chapters 7 and 9 illustrate the generalized dual problems of buying a vehicle in which to make the journey west and selling personal belongings to finance the trip. They show the uprooted tenant farmers being taken advantage of by shrewd sellers.

In the chapters immediately following, the Joads face these problems. Chapter 11 is a commentary on the dehumanization of the land which the tenants, now migrants, are leaving behind. The death of the houses and land, now separated from the people who cared for them, foreshadows the death of Grampa who is separated from his land.

We now meet Ma Joad, the strength and cohesive force of the Joad family. It is she who will live out Jim Casy's philosophy that all humanity is part of one thing. She will put his ideas of helping others into practice. Continuously she will think of humanity as one big family and help all those in need within her ability to do so. She is overjoyed when Tom arrives because, despite her fears she would never see him again, her family is now together around her and whole.

But Ma and Pa express an anxiety that will follow and concern Tom throughout the story. Their first reaction upon seeing him is that he broke out of jail and could be a problem for the family. As Muley Graves pointed out earlier, Tom's ability to act and help the family will be restricted because of his past and the terms of his parole.

In this unit two things happen to Tom. He moves from being a self-centered and self-protective individual to membership in a family unit. He is on his way to rejoining and uniting with all humanity. He is bound closer with Jim Casy, who also joins the family. Casy will have a profound effect on the development of Tom's character as the story progresses.

Here too is more development of Jim Casy's character. He wants to rejoin people after his long wandering. Symbolically he gives up his lone wandering and enters into the Joad family and participates in its decisions, a step toward being with and helping other people. Like Tom, he too is moving toward a participation in all mankind. Here he expresses the idea that everyone must help each other and breaks down a philosophical barrier when he tells Ma there is too much work to be done to divide it into "men's and women's work."

Casy is Steinbeck's voice for questioning old theologies and seeking a new and better world less bound by them. In this novel, which is essentially a Biblical allegory, Casy is a Christ-like figure, seeking the salvation of the downtrodden. He is also akin to Moses in leading them out of misery into a promised land. The migration of the "Dust Bowl" refugees is in great part an allegory of the Exodus of the Israelites from a land filled with pestilence to a land of milk and honey.

Grampa is the first to mention the "grapes" which symbolize the fertility of the new land and the expectation of a better, richer life that will grow and flourish in its soil. But Grampa is the first to perish in the quest for this good life. He is torn from the land he understands and which was his life force. As the land he left dies behind him, tended by men who do not love and understand it as he did, he too is dying as a result of being parted from it. As the story progresses, the other migrants will not find the bountiful life they seek and the only fruit that will grow in this new land is their wrath.

Ma expresses the first doubts about how promising the new land is, but maintains her confidence in the opportunity for work described in the handbills distributed among the tenants. Tom replies that he has heard things there are less desirable than advertised. This will later be heard from people they meet on the road who are returning dejectedly from California.

Deciding to take life day by day, the Joads set off with hope. The author of a recent nonfiction book about the migration has opined that the people involved were driven not so much by the pull of the promise offered by California as they were pushed by the desperate conditions behind them.

Study Questions

1. How did the used car salesmen take advantage of the farmers?

2. What is Ma and Pa Joad's first concern upon seeing Tom?

3. What is Ma's second concern about Tom?

4. What makes Ma Joad the core and strength of the family?

5. How does Jim Casy's behavior liken him to Jesus Christ?

6. Why did the farmers have to sell their tools and possessions for so little?

7. How do Ma and Tom feel about going to California just as the family is about to set off?

8. Why does Jim Casy ask to come along?

9. What does Ma do with the last few of her personal things, and why does she do it?

10. Why does Grampa change his mind about going to California?

Answers

1. They knew the farmers needed the cars and asked either high cash prices or high interest rates and sold anything they could get to operate through a variety of tricks, knowing they would not get complaints about the condition of the vehicles.

2. They are worried that Tom has broken out of jail, which would cause a problem for the family.

3. She is worried that jail may have made him "mean mad" like Pretty Boy Floyd and he will behave accordingly.

4. When she shows joy the family is happy. If she shows hurt they are sad. She is healer and arbiter and holds herself calm knowing that if she falters the family's will to go on would be lost.

5. The first sign we see of this is his questioning of the traditional religious ideas and his going off for years to wander and think things through. Then we see his desire to do something to help all people to a better life.

6. They could not take these things along and needed what money they could get for them to pay for gas and food on their journey, and the buyers, like the sellers of cars, took advantage of this to pay as little as possible.

7. They have some doubts about how good life will be there, but decide it is worthwhile to take life as it comes.

8. He wants to be among people again because he considers that holy in itself.

9. She picks out a very few things which seem to mean the most to her and burns the rest. She knew there was little room on the car made into a truck, and she had already insisted on taking the kitchen implements with which she could feed the family.

10. He just didn't want to leave what he considered his country, feeling he belonged there.

Suggested Essay Topics

1. Compare the behavior of the used car salesmen and the buyers of the belongings of the dispossessed farmers.

2. Discuss what the family council meeting, before they set out, tells about the way of life and culture of the Joads.

Unit III

Chapters 12–16

New Characters:

Ivy Wilson: *a farmer from Kansas, headed west, whose car has broken down along the highway*

Sarah Wilson: *his wife, who shows the strain of travel*

Summary

Chapter 12

Highway 66 was the main cross-country road running through Oklahoma and on west. On its long way it crossed mountains, dusty plains, more mountains, the arid south-western desert, and one final range of mountains before reaching the fertile green valleys of California. The migrants streamed from their former homes to the north and south of it and turned westward, forming small caravans of whatever vehicles they had been able to obtain.

When they needed parts to keep the vehicles moving, people along the way tried to take advantage of their plight and raised the price of the parts. If they charged much more than the four dollars a tire was worth, they considered it business. If the migrant took it for nothing, however, he was a thief. So the migrants would go on and try to make an old tire do until they could get a fairer price. Many times they had to walk long distances to get a needed part.

Chapter 13

After driving awhile, the Joads have to stop so Granma can go to the bathroom. They realize they have not brought any water with them, and Al says the truck needs gas also so they will stop at the next station and get both. The first thing the station attendant wants to know is if they have any money. This angers Al, but the man explains too many people are begging for gas or trading their meager possessions, even their shoes, for the gas to keep their vehicles moving west. He is bewildered by the number of people going west and asks what is happening to the country. Angrily Tom tells the attendant that although he asks that question, he, like many others, doesn't really want to know. Tom warns him that he too will be affected and driven out by the big company gas

stations. The man admits he has been considering leaving, and the family drives on.

Ma is worried that if Tom crosses the state line he will be in trouble because of his parole. He replies that he knows the chance he is taking, but it is better than staying where he is and starving.

After they turn onto Highway 66 Ma says they should stop before sunset so she can prepare food for them. Tom spots a good place to stop. There is a car there already and Tom asks the man by it if it is all right to stop there. The man replies he doesn't own the place, but only stopped there because his car couldn't go any further. He and his wife welcome the Joads to stop and share the place. They are Ivy and Sarah Wilson who have left their farm in Kansas to go west.

As Noah helps Grampa down off the truck, it is apparent that Grampa is not well. Mrs. Wilson offers to let him lie down in the tent they have put up. Once inside the tent Grampa has a stroke and dies. At a family council the Joads decide they will bury Grampa themselves, right there, according to their "own law," because they can't afford a regular funeral and don't want the authorities to put him in a pauper's grave. Mrs. Wilson helps Ma prepare the body in one of her quilts, which Ma offers to replace. All the men of the family dig a grave and ask Jim Casy to say a few words. Instead of praying over Grampa, Casy talks about the hard road ahead for the living. He says Grampa died when he was taken away from his farm and much need not be said about him because his life, whatever it had been, was done, but that the living were important.

The Wilsons tell of all the delays they have suffered caused by constant trouble with their car, with which Mr. Wilson does not know how to deal. Tom and Al promise to fix it. After looking at the car they suggest the two families distribute the people and baggage between the two vehicles and travel together. The Wilsons are happy to do so, although Mrs. Wilson is afraid it will be a burden on the Joads. Ma says it won't be a burden, that they will help each other.

Chapter 14

The great owners in the Western states did not realize the nature of the changes occurring, and they nervously resisted the changes. But those with the inborn desire to work and have meaningful lives plodded onward. For every step forward they might have to take a half step back, but they continued to push on. At first it was one man, one family, driven off the land, alone and bewildered. Families would camp together and "I lost my land" became "We lost our land." "I have a little food" and "I have none" became "We have a little food."

Chapter 15

There are eating places all along the road. Their favorite customers are the truck drivers who pay for their food, leave a tip, and bring other customers. The wealthy people who stop constantly complain and spend little. While two drivers are in one such place, an old car loaded with family possessions pulls in and the man in it asks for some water. He then asks if he can buy ten cents worth of bread. He only has a dime and a penny. Although bread is fifteen cents a loaf the cook tells the waitress to give him a loaf for ten cents. When the man's two sons look longingly at the candy in the counter the man asks if it costs a penny a piece. The waitress says it is two pieces for a penny. When the man and boys leave, the truck drivers say they know the candy is five cents a piece and they leave the waitress extra-large tips when they leave.

Chapter 16

Now joined together, the Joads and Wilsons cross the rest of Oklahoma and the Texas Panhandle. The road has become their home and movement their way of life. However, Rose of Sharon tells Ma of her and Connie's plan to settle in some town where Connie can find work and they can have a home of their own.

As they are crossing New Mexico, the Wilson's car breaks down again. Tom thinks it will take a day or two to fix. Pa refuses when Ivy Wilson tells the Joads to go on without them. Tom suggests the others all go on in the Joad truck and get work as soon as possible while he and Jim Casy stay and fix the car and catch up later. After all agree, Ma confronts Pa with a jack handle and refuses to let the family separate. The others give in to her.

Tom tells them to go find a nearby place for the night while he and Casy work on the car. Casy worries that so many

people are going west to look for work there won't be enough
work for all. Tom replies that he will cross that fence when
he comes to it, meanwhile putting one foot down at a time.
Al comes back in the truck and he and Tom go to a town for
the connecting rod needed to repair the car. At a wrecking
yard they find a one-eyed man who tells them to look around.
They find the right part, which the one-eyed man sells them
much more cheaply than he says his boss, whom he hates,
would. When the man relates all of his personal troubles and
feelings, Tom tells him to stop feeling sorry for himself and
do something to change his life for the better.

Tom and Al return to the car and fix it by the flashlight
the one-eyed man has also sold them very cheaply. They go
on to the campground where Al had left the family. The proprietor tells Tom it will be an extra fifty cents for the night
for the second car. He also says they will be arrested as va-
grants if they just stay at the side of the road. Tom starts to
argue when the proprietor calls him a bum, but Pa stops him.
Tom says he and Uncle John will take a chance on sleeping

in the car just off the road further on and watch for the family to catch up in the morning.

A raggedly dressed man standing nearby laughs when Pa talks about getting work and some land of their own in California. He says he has been there and is coming back. He tells them how the labor contractors advertise for more workers than they need, more than in fact there is work for, and pay the lowest wages they can to those who are starving and will work for anything they can get. His own wife and two children died of starvation he tells them. This worries Pa but Casy says what may be true for one man is not always true for another. As Tom leaves, he throws a clump of dirt at the proprietor who called him a bum.

Analysis

The previous unit ended with a description of the dying land being left behind. This unit opens with a shift of scene by describing the long and arduous road which the migrants must travel to begin to reach their goal of a better life. Throughout the novel the plot moves the action from scene to scene and from condition to condition. The main characters are carried along with the changes in scene and condition. Their conflict with the physical and social environment, more so than conflict between themselves, largely determines their actions. Whereas in the past they dealt with the loss of their homes and means of livelihood, now they will have to adjust to the trials of travel and the growing resistance of the people in the areas they enter.

As they move, the migrants will enter and impinge upon a society different than the one with which they have been familiar. As a matter of fact, the further they go, the more resistance they will encounter from the people whose places are already established in this new and different society. They will also receive kindness, however, from some of the people they encounter, who are, like themselves, working people. The road-stop waitress and cook, the truck drivers, and the one-eyed man in the wrecking yard are "good guys" who help, while those with wealth and position are pictured as the "bad guys." The one-eyed man in the wrecking yard is like the truck driver who earlier gave Tom a ride. Both are presented as poor employees who help other poor people because they resent their bosses whom they knew would not be as willing to do so. The camp proprietor represents still another class of people, those who take advantage of the migrants for their own profit. He points out that failure to pay his price, which Tom considers too high, will result in arrest for vagrancy if Tom tries to camp and sleep along the road for nothing. In the earlier intercalary chapter we encountered this theme. Those who charged too much for a tire were in business while the migrant who took the tire for nothing was a thief.

The joining of the Joad and Wilson families and the short intercalary chapter which follows carry forward some of the recurring themes of the story. First of these is Ma's thought that the poor must look to their own kind when they need help. In the banding together into a larger family, the concern shifts from the individual "I" to the communal "we" of a larger society. In "We have a little food," the reader hears an echo of Muley Graves sharing what little he had with those who had none.

In more of the allegory of the Exodus of the Israelites, the ragged man at the campground is like those sent out in advance by Moses who come back and give reports that the destination is not "a land of milk and honey" as promised.

For the first time we see Tom being aroused to action by conditions. He has been restraining his behavior by just putting one foot in front of the other and avoiding trouble, but he is angered at being considered a bum and is on the verge of physically fighting back. He has previously pointed out to the gas station attendant and the one-eyed man that they should take action to alleviate their troubles. And now resentment of the treatment he is receiving is pushing him to action. His throwing the clump of dirt at the proprietor is the first step in his change from being a solitary, docile prison inmate to a member of a group fighting against oppressors.

The theme of family unity and strength appears in this unit in two different ways: the death of Grampa and the joining with the Wilsons. The first is part of the breaking up of the small Joad family. This will continue throughout the rest of the novel. Grampa's death also is an occasion for the Joads to act according to their traditional family codes. They bury their own dead with respect and, as a once independent farm family, they refuse to accept a pauper's grave for him or charity from others for themselves. Their joining with the Wilsons represents the social evolution from the single family to the group of families that help each other through adversity. Casy's idea, that all people are part of one big thing and that people need each other, is beginning to be shown. This idea will be further developed in future chapters by the joining together of ever larger groups of families, even in the temporary camps, for the good of all.

Grampa's death also lets us see more of Casy's concern for the living and their struggles. We see this again in his worry that there may not be enough work in California for all who want it.

Finally, in this unit we see the beginning of another change in the Joad family. With Grampa's death Pa becomes the head of the family, but he is almost immediately challenged by Ma when she confronts him and insists the family not be separated.

Study Questions

1. How does Steinbeck compare what actions are considered to be business and what is considered to be thievery in Chapter 12?

2. Why does the gas station attendant resent the big company stations in town?

3. How do the Joads and Wilsons help each other?

4. For what three reasons do the Joads decide to bury Grampa themselves?

5. How does Chapter 14 herald the formation of a new society, with a new attitude among the migrants?

6. How do the people in this unit represent the "haves" and "have nots" in American society during the depression?

7. Why doesn't Ma want the truck to go on ahead when the Wilsons' car breaks down again?

8. What worries Jim Casy about so many people going west?

9. How is the one-eyed man in the auto parts lot like the truck driver who gave Tom a ride earlier in the story?

10. How does the ragged man's warning coincide with Casy's worry about the availability of work in California?

Answers

1. He says charging people more than a thing is worth is considered business while taking what is needed without paying for it is considered theft.

2. The big companies get customers who spend more, but his customers beg for gas or want to trade items he can't use.

3. The Wilsons give hospitality and shelter, and help when Grampa dies, and in turn the Joads fix the Wilsons' car.

4. They don't have enough money for a funeral, they are too proud to have him given a pauper's grave, and burying their own kin has been traditional for them.

5. It signals the change from "I" to "we" in dealing with problems and foreshadows a self-governing solidarity among the migrants.

6. The wealthy are pictured as either uncaring or willing to take advantage of the plight of the migrants while those of the working class, who are closer to the migrants economically, extend the help that is needed.

7. Ma's greatest fear is having the family break apart, and she wants nothing done to separate them.

8. He is afraid there will not be enough jobs for them all and something awful will happen.

9. He is willing to break the rules set by the boss he dislikes and give help to people who need it.

10. He says that there is not enough work for all the people streaming west, employers pay wages that are not enough to live on, and conditions for the migrants are awful.

Suggested Essay Topics

1. Describe and comment on the emerging changes in Tom Joad's character as shown in his behavior with the gas station man, the one-eyed man, and the camp proprietor.

2. Explain and illustrate the ways in which Ma Joad's character remains essentially unchanged, with one exception, as she is confronted with new situations.

Unit IV

Chapters 17–21

New Character:

Floyd Knowles: *a migrant having trouble finding work*

Summary

Chapter 17

Day by day the migrants moved westward along the highway, clustering each night where there was water and company. Each camp became a temporary world for the night and "twenty families became one family." A form of self-government grew up. Out of the respect for law and order they brought from their old homes, the migrants established rules of conduct and of rights among themselves, and the rules became laws. Any violator of these laws was expelled from the group. Evenings were spent in making friends and talking about their homes and their future. There might even be some singing, but mainly they rested to be ready for the next day's travel.

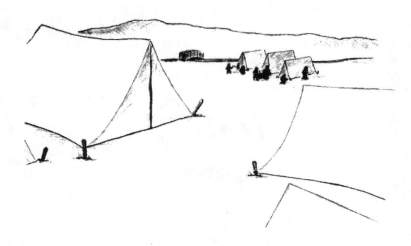

Chapter 18

At the Arizona border a guard asks the Joads where they are going and how long they will be in Arizona, and he tells them they had better keep moving. They drive on and stop just across the Colorado River, the California border. The first person they talk to warns them a cop will be down to "look them over." They decide they need some rest before crossing the desert ahead.

The men go to the river and sit in its coolness. A man and boy join them. The man says they are on their way back because he can't make a living in California. When Pa asks about work there, the man describes poor conditions. He remarks that a lot of good land is not farmed because the owners don't want to farm it. He also says the people of California are afraid of the migrant workers who they know are hungry and desperate. From him they first hear the term "Okie," by which the local people mean a "dirty son-of-a-bitch."

They decide to cross the desert in the cool of the night.

Down by the river, Noah tells Tom he is going to stay by the river and catch fish. He says a fellow can't starve beside a nice river. When Tom cannot change his mind and convince him to stay with the family, Noah wanders off down the river.

Granma appears to be delirious, talking to Grampa. A woman holds a religious meeting for her despite Ma's refusal of her offer. A policeman tells Ma they had better not be there another day. When she confronts him angrily, he tells her he does not want any "goddamn Okies settling down." Later Tom tells Ma what the word "Okie" means to the cop. When he tells her about Noah, Ma feels the "family's fallin' apart."

They get ready to depart and Ivy Wilson tells them his wife can go no farther. Despite the cop's warning to be gone by morning, Ma thinks about waiting until they can all go

together. Wilson says they must go on and asks Jim Casy to see Mrs. Wilson. She asks Casy to say a prayer, but he cannot. She knows she is dying of cancer but doesn't want her husband to know. Over Mr. Wilson's protest the Joads leave him two dollars and some meat and they start out to cross the desert.

At a border control station an officer starts to inspect all the contents of the truck. Ma tells him there is a very sick old woman inside who must get to a doctor quickly and he lets them pass. However, when they get to the next town Ma says Granma does not need a doctor. After an all night drive across the desert they reach the last mountains before their destination. Ma tells them Granma was dead before they reached the control station, and she lied because the family had to get across the desert.

Chapter 19

The landowners in California were descended from Americans who had taken the land away from the Mexicans who owned it. Starting as squatters, they made their living from the land and began to consider it theirs. As they acquired more and more land they turned farming into an industry, hired overseers and imported foreign laborers to do the actual work.

When the great migration from the dust bowl began, the owners became frightened that, if allowed to become squatters, the migrants would try to take over ownership of the land. So they tried to keep wages low and hired guards to protect their property. But the migrants kept coming, bringing their dreams of a better life with them.

Chapter 20

The Joads, once again unable to afford a proper funeral, leave Granma's body with a local coroner for burial. They find

a camping place at the edge of town. The first man they speak to answers incoherently. Another man explains the first has been pushed around by too many cops and is now "bull-simple."

The man tells them three or four times as many people as the handbills say are needed show up for work and the wages were cut. Yet there are many with hungry children who will work for the low wages. When Tom asks why the migrants don't organize, the man says that anyone who talks about organizing is arrested as a troublemaker. Tom is disgusted by this. The man tells Tom the cops expect Okies to act "bull-simple" and cautions him to do so to avoid trouble.

Casy and Tom talk and Casy wonders how he can repay the Joads and what he can do to make life better for all of the migrant people.

Rose of Sharon tells Connie she is sick and they must have a house before the baby is born. Connie says they should have stayed in Oklahoma where he could have learned to operate a tractor. He leaves the tent and walks away.

Ma cooks a stew with the first meat the family has had in days. Several children gather around and watch her hungrily. One offers to keep the fire going, and tells Ma about a government camp for migrants that is better than this one. Ma doesn't know what to do about the hungry children because she hasn't enough food for her own family. However, she leaves a little stew in the pot and tells the children they can each have one taste. She hurries into the tent so she won't see them digging in the pot with sticks. The mother of one of the children tells Ma she is causing trouble by giving them the stew, but Ma replies that even though she didn't have enough for her own family, because of the way the children looked at her, she couldn't keep it from them.

Floyd Knowles, the man who earlier spoke with Tom, tells Al the men in the camp have scanned the area for any type of work but there is none to be had. Floyd tells Al and Tom there is supposed to be work hundreds of miles further north. A man drives into the camp and says he needs workers in Tulare, and when Floyd asks how much it pays, the man says it depends. When Floyd wants a contract stating the wage before he will come, the labor contractor calls a deputy. Floyd says if the contractor were "on the level" he wouldn't need a deputy. The deputy arrests Floyd, accusing him of breaking into a used car lot. When Tom speaks up the deputy threatens to arrest him too. He then warns them he will have the camp burned down if they don't go to Tulare. Floyd runs, the

deputy starts after him, and Tom trips the deputy. Casy kicks the deputy in the neck. He reminds Tom about his parole and tells him to hide. He takes the blame when more deputies arrive. The first one is not sure Casy is the right man, but he is arrested and taken away.

Uncle John says he needs to get drunk and gets money from Pa. Tom comes out of hiding and the family packs its belongings. Rose of Sharon asks where Connie is and Tom tells her he saw Connie walking away from the camp. Then he goes after Uncle John and finds him in a ditch refusing to move. Tom knocks him out and carries him back to the truck.

Expecting trouble as they leave, Ma urges Tom to be careful. He replies he is getting mad because the cops are "tryin' to break us." He says, "They're working on our decency." Ma cautions him to stay out of trouble and he says he will try but that the cops' actions are not legal.

As they approach a town, there is a mob blockading the road. A deputy tells Tom to turn around and go back. He says, "We ain't gonna have no goddamn Okies in this town." Restraining himself, Tom turns the truck around but soon drives off the road and circles the town continuing in the direction he wanted to go. He says to Ma, "We can still go where we want, even if we got to crawl for the right." Ma says to have patience, that "us people will go on livin' when all them people is gone."

Chapter 21

The people who had lived all their lives on just 40 acres were now migrants. The highway, the camps, the hunger and fear of hunger, and the endless moving changed them. And the hostility they met changed them. There was panic among the inhabitants of the land they entered, and they became hostile to the migrants. They armed to repel the invaders. People who had never known hunger or want now saw hunger and want in the eyes of the migrants and gathered to defend themselves and what was theirs. They formed armed units, convincing themselves that they were good and the invaders were bad. The men in these units, clerks and storekeepers, did not own land but feared competing for the jobs they had with hungry men. And the migrants fought for what work there was, working for less than the next man just to get something.

The great owners of the land created a new system to keep wages low and prices high. They controlled both by selling their fruit to their own canneries below cost and by keeping the cost of canned fruit high. The small farmers lost their land to the great owners and the banks and they joined the migrant hungry. The great companies did not recognize the thin line between hunger and anger and continued to use their money for guns and repressive measures instead of paying better wages.

Analysis

The intercalary chapters in this unit are concerned with the sub-society the migrants established among themselves and the resistance to their coming by the larger society they were entering.

The migrants merged into groups larger than single families, with agreed upon rules of behavior which had the practical force of laws among them. They were a people with a heritage of order and of obeying laws they understood and respected.

They were entering a society controlled by a very few who owned most of the farming land and controlled those who owned only small farms. Migrant labor was not new to this society, but in the past it had consisted of Orientals and Mexicans. The new migrants were old-stock Americans who posed a threat by wanting to own part of the land as they had where they came from. Thus the large owners became frightened, kept wages low, and hired guards to protect their property as well as policemen to coerce and control the migrants. But they didn't understand the real danger, which was the Okie's strong faith in each other and their persistence to keep trying for better conditions.

The fright and resistance went beyond the large owners, corporations, and banks to the small farmers, shopkeepers, and working people. They were afraid of the competition for jobs from the increasing numbers of hungry people willing to work cheaply, and they organized and armed themselves to resist the ever-growing tide of Okies who they convinced themselves were bad.

This, then, is what the Joads find as they near the end of

their long overland journey. The plot has again moved the action to a new scene and new conditions. Their conflict with the new social and economic environment will again determine their actions, even giving rise to some conflicts between themselves as to how to deal with this environment.

At the first stopping place in California, they are made aware of the hostile attitude of the established residents when they hear the word "Okie" and learn the derogatory manner in which it is applied to them. The attitude is implicit in the way the policeman speaks to Ma. She reacts angrily to this, as does Tom to the meaning of "Okie."

In this unit Tom's anger grows, and he takes a few first steps in the direction in which he eventually will go to fight back against the harshness of the treatment of the migrants. He resents and rebels against being told where to go and what to do by the cops and the local mob. From the loner who put down one foot at a time and avoided trouble, he is starting to think about the migrants organizing to combat the conditions. He is moving ever closer to being involved in the troubles and struggles of people other than himself.

The scene and conditions also cause Tom to take two direct responsive actions. He physically intervenes when Floyd Knowles is about to be falsely arrested for demanding better terms from the labor contractor. Later, he circumvents the roadblock he perceives as another illegal attack on the decency of the migrants.

At the river, the Joads hear again about the poor working and living conditions ahead of them and the attitude of the inhabitants. Rather than face further trials, Noah goes off by himself.

Ma realizes this is the beginning of the disintegration of the Joad family that she is so committed to keeping together. As they become more impoverished, more of the family will leave it. First, they have to abandon the Wilsons who have become part of the family, and then Granma dies. But even in Granma's death Ma shows her own strength and devotion to the family by lying about Granma so the family can get across the desert to the land which they dream of reaching. Not only is the family disintegrating but its standards are also deteriorating. Once considering themselves independent and asking no charity, they now have to commit Granma to the pauper's grave they so dreaded for Grampa.

Arriving in California represents the achievement of a dream for the Joads. But now they find the dream shattered, and the ugliness, filth, and disorder of the first camp they stop at represents the further deterioration in their lives. They learn the work they had been hoping for is not to be had. Connie deserts Rose of Sharon. Jim Casy is lost from the family when he steps forward and takes the blame for Tom's trouble with the deputy and enables Tom to stay with them.

Thus, like Tom, Casy also takes action. Until now he has been merely a thinker trying to solve his own dilemmas and formulate a way to solve those of others. Now, he is a doer. He sees a way to repay the Joads for their kindness to him and does so by sacrificing himself for what he sees as their good. He is now on his way to devoting himself to action that will benefit all of the people of the whole human family he believes to be holy.

Ma again gives life to his principles by feeding the hungry children of her neighbors even when she doesn't have enough food for her own smaller family. And later she expresses Casy's faith in the people to go on in the face of adversity.

Study Questions

1. What good thing happened when the migrants stopped for the night along the highway, and why?

2. What is the first warning of trouble the Joads receive when they arrive in California?

3. What attitude of the California residents does the cop at the river represent?

4. How does the man at the river echo the ragged man at the roadside camp?

5. Why did Ma keep Granma's death a secret at the inspection station?

6. Why didn't the migrants organize to obtain better working and living conditions?

7. What promise of better living did the young girl indicate to Ma was available at the government camps?

8. How does Casy explain taking the blame for Floyd and Tom after the fight with the deputy?

9. How did the California landowners react to the Okies?

10. What is Tom Joad's reaction to his first encounters with the people of California?

Answers

1. They formed larger groups of families in temporary communities and established laws to preserve order and their rights because they were basically good, law-abiding people.

2. They are told they will be checked out by the police.

3. He tells them he doesn't want them "settling down." This is echoed later when the deputy tells them Okies were not wanted in the town.

4. He is returning to his home having been defeated by the miserable conditions in California.

5. She knew the family had to get across the desert that

   night, and like Casy, considered the needs of the living
   important.

6. Anybody who even talked about organizing was arrested as a troublemaker, as was Floyd Knowles for
   even questioning the motives of the labor contractor.

7. She said they were clean and had running water and
   toilets.

8. He said someone had to take the blame and he could
   handle it, but that Tom had broken parole and could
   be sent back to prison which would be trouble for Ma
   and Pa.

9. The landowners were frightened by the migrants and
   hired men to protect their interests and control the
   Okies.

10. He is aroused and starts to take action to fight back
    against their treatment of the Okies.

Suggested Essay Topics

1. Describe the different ways the migrants banded together along the highway and became a cohesive society.

2. Compare the social and economic conditions the migrant families encountered in the California farm
   country with the conditions in the places they left.

Unit V
Chapters 22–26

New Characters:

Jim Rawley: *the manager of a camp where the migrants govern themselves and living conditions are much better*

Ezra Huston: *a migrant who heads the Central Committee, the group of people who regulate conduct in the camp*

Summary

Chapter 22

The Joads go to a camp provided for the migrants by the Federal government where there is one vacant spot they can occupy. Tom learns that cops can't come into this camp unless there is major trouble or they have a warrant, and the migrants elect their own police and make their own laws.

The next morning Tom meets the Wallaces. They invite him to breakfast and offer to take him to a farm where they have found work digging ditches. The farmer, his land mortgaged, has to pay less than he has been paying or be in trouble with the Farmer's Association and the bank who dictate the wages he pays. Being sympathetic to the Okies, he secretly warns them some people will start trouble at the camp dance on Saturday to give the deputies an excuse to enter and break up the camp. The landowners fear the migrants are getting used to being treated too well in the camp and will be harder to control when they move to other camps run by the owners.

Ma is delighted with the running water and wash tubs, showers, and toilets and is happy to be able to clean up to meet the Ladies Committee for the Joad's section of the camp. She talks with Jim Rawley, the camp manager, and realizes he and the inhabitants of the camp are her kind of good people. Ma and Rose of Sharon meet the committee and learn the camp's routines and rules and how the really destitute can get food on credit until work is found.

Pa, Al, and Uncle John go looking for work, but all they

find are signs saying, "No Help Wanted. No Trespassing."
Another man from the camp tells them he has searched for
a week without finding work. Pa is depressed but Ma is op-
timistic because Tom found work and says something will
turn up if he looks further.

Chapter 23

The migrants searched frantically for some kind of work,
scraped and scrabbled to live, and found what pleasure they
could in humble activities. They created pleasures with what
little they had: their remaining sense of humor, tales of earlier days or their ancestors, and musical instruments they
had brought along. Some would spend a part of their little
money to see a movie and then entertain the others telling
about it. With a little money some would seek escape in drink
and dreams of pleasant experiences. Others found pleasure
in having a preacher tell them they were cleansed of sin,
while wishing they knew what sins they could do.

Chapter 24

Preparations for the dance start early on Saturday. Ezra
Huston, the head of the Central Committee, says he has
added extra people to the committee to quietly stop any
trouble. The migrants are mystified as to why the landowners want to destroy the camp. Tom is told to stay at the main
gate with another man to check arriving guests and keep
troublemakers out. Three men who say a Mr. Jackson invited
them arouse suspicion. Jackson says he had worked with
them at a farm but did not invite them to the dance. The
committee watches the three and waits. Things go well until
one of the three insists on dancing with someone else's girl.
The committee quietly surrounds and moves the trio off the
dance floor. But somewhere someone has blown a whistle
and a carload of deputies drive up and demand entrance

because they hear a riot inside. When all they can hear is quiet music they leave but wait nearby.

Huston doesn't understand why some migrants are turning against their own people. One says "a fella gotta eat" but will say no more about who sent them nor admit to being paid. They are put over the back fence without being harmed and with a warning that anybody attempting such a thing again will be severely beaten.

Later that night, another migrant tells of some mountain people hired as cheap labor who organized when the local townspeople bought guns and gasoline. He says 5,000 mountain men, each armed with a rifle, walked through the town and the people left them alone. He says they called it a

"Turkey Shoot" and thinks the migrants should have a Turkey Shoot.

Chapter 25

In California a great deal of food was growing. Scientists had devised many ways to make the fruit and vegetables bigger, better, and more abundant. However, much of it was going to waste. The small farmers could not get enough money from the canneries to pay to have their crops harvested. Soon their small orchards and vineyards would belong to the corporation or the bank. Only those who owned the canneries would survive, because they bought cheaply and kept prices high and because canned produce would last for years. Some of the abundant food was destroyed to keep the prices high. Those who needed and could have eaten and been nourished by the surplus were not allowed to use it. Much was just allowed to decay and the smell of decay spread over the state. Among the hungry, wrath was growing.

Chapter 26

Ma tells the men something has to be done, and they are afraid to talk about it. She points out they have little food and no money left and that only Tom has found what little work there was. Pa doesn't want to leave because the camp is so nice, but Ma tells him they can't eat niceness. The men can't decide where to go, but Ma insists they go the very next morning anyway. Pa remarks to Tom that it used to be that the men said what would be done but that now the women were saying it. Ma tells Tom she made Pa mad to keep him going on.

Rose of Sharon once again expresses worry over the effect all the troubles will have on her unborn baby, but Ma cheers her up. Pa says goodbye to some men, and Tom and his friends talk about organizing.

The Joads are up before dawn and leave the camp. Ma tells Tom they must have a house before winter. While they are fixing a flat tire on the truck, a man comes by and tells them there is work picking peaches only 35 miles away. Hoping to get some work that day, they drive on and talk about what they will buy with the money they will earn.

They are met by cops who say they will earn five cents for each box of peaches they pick. The cops escort the Joads into a fenced area past a throng of shouting people who look like migrants. Tom asks about the people and is told to mind his own business. The Joads unload the truck at the shed assigned to them and the four men immediately go to the peach orchard to start work.

The first box of peaches Tom picks are rejected because the manager says they are bruised. He has to start over and it takes longer to pack the peaches in the boxes carefully. Ruthie, Winfield, and then Ma, come to help and together all seven members of the family earn a total of one dollar for the day's work. Ma finds prices at the company store are higher than in town and the dollar doesn't buy enough to feed the family. When she asks the clerk to give her some sugar on credit against the next day's wages, he says he can't. He pays for the sugar himself. Ma repeats that, "If you're in trouble or hurt or need, go to the poor people. They're the only ones that'll help." She points out that although they have eaten what cost them their total day's pay they are still hungry.

Tom goes to see what the trouble is outside the fence but a guard won't let him through the gate. He goes down the fence and slips under it. Outside he meets Jim Casy, who tells him how the prisoners in his jail all started yelling at the same time and got better food. Casy is now trying to organize the migrants so things will get better. He says those outside the fence went on strike when the wages were cut in half and are now being badly mistreated. Tom tells him how things were in the government camp and Casy says he wants things that way everywhere. Casy knows the wages will be cut in half again the next day now that more people are there to pick the peaches.

Some men approach. Tom and Casy try to get away but are chased and stopped. As Casy tells them "You don't know what you're doing," one of them crushes his head with a pick handle and kills him. Enraged, Tom kills the man with the same weapon. After being struck himself, he manages to get away, hide, and get back into the camp.

In the morning he tells the Joads he must leave. Ma says no. She tells him he needs protection and the members of the family are the only ones he can trust to hide him. They pick enough peaches that day to buy gas and that night they hollow out a hiding place for Tom in the truck and leave the camp. They see a sign that offers work picking cotton. Tom tells his parents that he will hide in a culvert near the cotton field while they get work.

Analysis

In this unit the movement of plot from scene to scene and condition to condition continues and the conflict between the Okies and the vested interests grows.

The first movement is from the conditions of filth, disorder, and fear of cops in Hooverville to the cleanliness, order, and confidence in the committee form of government in the Weedpatch camp. Tom relaxes without more cops to face. He finds fellowship with men willing to share their food as well as the little work to be found. Ma feels she is once again among her own kind of people who behave in ways to which she is accustomed. Pa does not want to leave when it becomes necessary because the camp is so nice. But the camp's promise of hope is fleeting and illusionary for the Joads. They are still migrants and do not find in Weedpatch the type of home Ma wants nor the meaningful work Pa needs. Soon the hope fades and the Joads must move on to the conditions of the hunger and squalor of migratory life in the peach orchard.

It is Ma who recognizes and reacts to the conditions. She knows they can't continue to live in Weedpatch with little food and no money or work. It is at this point she starts to take over the management of the family and goads the men into action. Pa and Uncle John have been weakened by not having the dignity of having men's work to do which once gave them the position as the head of the family. Ma still has her woman's work of feeding and caring for the family. Still having her work, she is more in control of herself and her position is stronger, so she begins to assume leadership. When Tom kills a man, it is she who makes the decision for the family to leave the peach camp and hide him. She feels she has to take this control because Pa has lost it and there can be no family without it.

This unit also offers some commentaries on the character of the Okies. The Wallaces demonstrate that the willingness to share with one another is a common trait among them and not just solely one of Ma Joad's. The Ladies Committee embodies the willingness to cooperate and help each other. An intercalary chapter and the camp dance show their enjoyment of simple social gatherings. And there are examples of their desire and ability to have a sense of order in their living together in community.

The idea of organization, which Tom earlier brought up with Floyd Knowles, is enlarged in this unit. In Weedpatch the migrants demonstrate their ability to organize themselves and work well and efficiently in achieving their goals when left on their own. The way they handle the attempt to destroy the camp carries the idea forward. It gives a picture of advantages organization would give them in dealing with the treatment they are receiving at the hands of the large landowners, labor contractors, and deputies. This is exactly the reason the owners fear them and try to destroy the good way of life in the camps and break any attempted strikes. The owners have created a system of agriculture that they ruthlessly control for their benefit. There is an undercurrent here that the owners realize they may not be able to control what they themselves have created by luring the migrant labor to California.

But there are signs that organizing to openly fight the owners and their minions is in the minds of the Okies and is growing alongside the growing wrath over the conditions they are enduring: witness the recommendation for the Tur-key Shoot and the strike at the peach orchard. We now see Jim Casy, who has been inspired by what the concerted ef-fort by a whole group can do, and is actively trying to orga-nize the migrants as his new calling for doing good for mankind. In his death in pursuit of his efforts on behalf of oppressed people, he again appears as a Christ figure. Steinbeck even has him say to his killers, the oppressors, "You don't know what you're doing."

The death of his friend breaks Tom's restraint and he kills in return. He has killed before, but that was because he had been injured. This time he kills because a fellow man has been violated. He is nearing the end of his personal journey from lone individual to membership in the family of man-kind. But he must now go into hiding and can no longer help his own small family. Instead he becomes a burden on them which forces them to move on to a new scene and new con-ditions.

Study Questions

1. Why don't the police and deputies harass the people in the Weedpatch camp?

2. What makes the farmer named Thomas lower the wages he has paid to the Wallaces?

3. How does the government camp differ from the "Hoovervilles"?

4. What things does the Saturday night dance tell about the character of the migrants?

5. What kind of men are the three who come to the dance to cause trouble?

6. How does the camp committee forestall the deputies who are poised to enter the camp the night of the dance?

7. Why do the Joads leave Weedpatch and move to the peach field?

8. What is Ma's big disappointment the first day the family picks peaches?

9. Why were all the people shouting outside the fence?

10. Why is Jim Casy killed?

Answers

1. It is Federal government property that they can only enter with a warrant for a wanted criminal or to quell a riot.

2. The wages he pays are set, and dictated to him, by the Farmer's Association and the bank which holds his mortgage.

3. It is clean and well-regulated and has facilities for decent living.

4. It shows they enjoy social life and music and, when organized and well led, they can deal with trouble efficiently.

5. They are themselves migrant workers who have been turned against their own kind of people because they are hungry.

6. They stop trouble before it can begin and remove the reason the deputies can use to enter and destroy the camp.

7. They can't support themselves in Weedpatch and on their way to possible work they learn of a chance to earn desperately needed money before their gas runs out.

8. All the money the whole family made working hard

that day did not buy enough food and they were still hungry.

9. They had gone on strike when the wages were cut in half and were protesting because new people were going in to do the work making their strike a failure.

10. He is trying to organize the migrant workers which is what the landowners fear most.

Suggested Essay Topics

1. Describe and explain the effect the migration from the Dust Bowl had on the different classes of people already living in California.

2. Describe how the behavior in the stops along the highway was later reflected in the government camp.

Unit VI

Chapters 27–30

New Characters:

Mr. and Mrs. Wainwright: *migrants who have little left but their pride who share living space in a boxcar with the Joads*

Aggie Wainwright: *their daughter who will marry Al Joad*

Summary

Chapter 27

There was cotton to be picked and willing hands to pick it. The wages weren't bad and they knew cotton, having picked it back home. They bought a collecting bag and paid for it with the first part of their labor. It was hard, tiring work. They dragged the big bag and filled it. Even the kids helped fill it. And they talked and sang as they worked. The bag got heavy. They got paid by the weight. The boss said they put rocks in it, and they said his scale was crooked. Each was right at times. It was good work, with money and meat at the end of each day. But there were thousands arriving to do the work of hundreds and the fields were picked clean rapidly. And winter was coming fast and there would be no work then.

Chapter 28

Being among the first to reach the cotton field, the Joads get to live in one-half of a boxcar rather than a tent. With the money they earn, they are able to buy new clothes and eat meat every night. But when Ma buys some Cracker Jacks as a special treat for Ruthie and Winfield, Ruthie gets into a fight over them with another girl. She threatens the girl by telling her about Tom killing two men and hiding nearby.

When Ma learns of this, she immediately goes to meet Tom. He takes her to the cave where he has been hiding. Ma tells him he has to leave and asks what he will do. Tom says that hiding had given him a lot of time to think. He has been thinking about Casy's idea about everyone being part of one big soul and one man's little piece of the soul wasn't so good unless the rest was whole.

Tom feels he has to finish the work Casy started, so he will try to organize the people. When Ma reminds him Casy was killed, Tom says he will duck faster than Casy did. When Ma wonders if she will ever see him again, Tom tells her she will see him everywhere around her, anywhere people are in need or trouble or fighting for a better life.

On her way back to the boxcar Ma meets a man who says he needs people to pick the cotton on his small 20 acres the next day. He tells her of his problems with The Association setting wages. When she gets back, the Wainwrights, who share the boxcar, tell the Joads they are worried about Al getting Aggie, their daughter, pregnant and possibly bringing shame on them. Ma says Pa or she will speak to Al. Later

Pa tells Ma he isn't any good anymore. All he can do is think about the home he'll never see again. He says, "We got nothin' now," and "Seems like our life's over and done." But Ma refuses to believe this and says they will go on.

Al tells them he and Aggie are going to get married and live in a town where he will get a job working on cars. The two families celebrate together and decide to go pick the cotton together. They get there early but so do many other people and the field is picked clean before noon. By the time they get back to the boxcar, rain is pouring down and Rose of Sharon is having chills.

Chapter 29

Grey clouds formed over the mountains and the rains began slowly and then increased. Water collected in puddles, then ponds, and then lakes in low places. Rivers and streams flowed over their banks. The flood engulfed the tent homes and the cars. The people sought higher ground and crowded there in despair. Men and boys went out and begged or stole food, not even running if shot at. The women watched the men for signs of a break again. They saw fear turning to anger. They knew that, as long as this turn from fear to wrath continued, the break would never come.

Chapter 30

Al covers the motor of the truck as the rains continue. The Joads and Wainwrights, now one family, wonder if they should leave but since they are still dry and Rose of Sharon is getting sicker, Pa decides to build an embankment to hold back the flood waters and goes to get other men to help.

He returns and finds Rose of Sharon in the labor of childbirth. He tells the men that for this reason they must build the embankment. They work frantically into the night as the water rises. They succeed in blocking it until a tree is uprooted and punches a hole in the bank and the water floods the entire area. Al rushes to move the truck but it will not start and has to be abandoned in the flood waters.

Rose of Sharon's baby is stillborn. Pa wonders what he could have done. When he goes out, Mrs. Wainwright comes over to give Ma some rest. The women talk about helping each other and Ma says, "Use' ta be the fambly was first. It ain't so now. It's anybody. Worse off we get, the more we got to do."

Pa, Al, and Uncle John gauge the water to see if it will flood the boxcar. They use part of the truck bed to build a platform above the floor. Mrs. Wainwright asks them to bury the dead child. While it is against the law for them to do it, they can't do anything else. Uncle John starts to bury it and then just lets it float away in the stream.

Pa gets some bread and bacon for breakfast and tells Ma he spent all the money they had left for it. They all huddle on the platform as water covers the boxcar floor. The next day Pa brings 10 potatoes. They eat these and spend another night.

The next day Ma decides it is time to go. She tells Al, who is going to stay with Aggie, to watch their belongings until they can return. With Pa carrying Rose of Sharon, Uncle John carrying Ruthie, and Ma carrying Winfield, they wade through the flood waters.

Ma sees a barn that she thinks will be dry and they go to it. In the barn they find dry hay and also discover a boy huddling over a man lying on his back. The boy tells them that his father is starving, and when he stole some bread his father vomited it up. He says the father needs soup or milk. Ma takes the wet clothing off of Rose of Sharon and wraps her in a dry blanket she gets from the boy. She looks at Rose of Sharon with a question in her eyes and Rose understands and nods her agreement. Ma takes the others out of the barn

and Rose of Sharon puts the dying man's head to her milk-filled breasts.

Analysis

Chapter 27 moves the action again to a new place and sets the scene for what the Joads will experience while picking cotton. Conditions are somewhat improved. There is a respite from hunger. However, this will not last because there are still more people than the available work requires.

As their condition grows worse, the Joad family disintegration continues. Tom leaves and Al announces he soon will too.

With winter coming there will be no more work for the Joads. Thus nature, as it was in the beginning, becomes their hostile environment. Once again severe weather conditions drive them from a home. The drought caused by lack of enough rain began their troubles and set them on their long, arduous journey and their struggles to find a good life. This time it is heavy rains and flooding that drive them out. In fact, the flood takes what little else they have left. The truck becomes as useless as their farming implements had and it too has to be abandoned. They are in a final desperate struggle just to survive.

Tom will enter a great struggle of his own choosing. Earlier Jim Casy asked him to go among the people in the peach orchard and talk to them about what was happening and what could be done. Though his wrath was growing like that of all the migrants, he was not then fully ready to be Casy's emissary. But now he too has been in the wilderness thinking, and has come to understand and adopt Casy's idea that all men are part of one big thing and need to be together. He has completed his personal journey from self-interested individual to member of a family to part of the whole of humanity. Now he feels he must go out and organize the whole for the good of all. He will be the disciple who takes Casy's idealism and puts it into action.

Tom, having just come out of the prison, had refused to sleep in a cave on the old Joad farm. Having killed again, he hides in the thicket which is as dark as a cave. It is here that he comes to his decision to carry on Casy's work. His emergence from this womb-like cave, with a new direction to his life, can be seen as a symbolic rebirth for him.

Rose of Sharon's stillborn baby can be seen as a symbol of her stillborn dream of a nice house and family. Further, it can symbolize the lack of fruition of the dreams of the Joad family for the better life they have traveled so far to find.

Ma echoes Tom and Casy when she tells Mrs. Wainwright that now everybody is important, not just her own family and, like Tom, she expresses the idea that the poor people will go on and survive the struggle by standing together. Her belief, and Tom's determination to get the common people to stand together, offer a hope for the future.

There are other rays of hope. The men find something they can do that is worthwhile and take action together to build a wall against the flood. The women see the signs of anger that indicate the men will not break. Al and Aggie will try to fulfill the dreams Connie and Rose of Sharon had. And in a final act of sharing, Rose of Sharon accepts Ma's suggestion and performs an act usually done in the intimacy of the family to give life to a fellow human being in need.

Study Questions

1. What is the significance of the arguments over the weight of the cotton the migrants picked?

2. How do the Joads benefit from getting to the cotton field ahead of many others?

3. Do other conditions improve for the Joads when they get work picking cotton?

4. What makes it necessary for Tom to break away from the family?

5. Why is the 20 acres of cotton picked so quickly?

6. Why were the migrant women relieved when they saw the faces of the men after all the troubles?

7. What does Mr. Wainwright's worry about Al and Aggie reveal about him and his way of life?

8. What do Rose of Sharon's stillborn baby and Al and Aggie's engagement symbolize?

9. What is a final crushing blow to the Joads' dreams?

10. What does Rose of Sharon nursing the dying man symbolize?

Answers

1. Each side, bosses and migrants, thought the other was trying to cheat them.

2. They get a sturdier place to live than a tent and good neighbors to share it with.

3. Yes, they finally get enough money to eat more and better food and replace worn clothing.

4. Since he killed the deputy, he is a danger to the family, and Ruthie gives away the fact that he is wanted and nearby.

5. There are so many people seeking work, more migrants come to the small farm than are needed and no one gets enough work.

6. They saw the men were angry rather than defeated and would not break under the weight of the troubles.

7. He is trying to cling to his pride in never having shame brought on his family.

8. The baby symbolizes the stillborn dreams of all the Joads, while the engagement symbolizes the hope that some of them might yet be achieved.

9. The flood robs them of the simple home they have been able to create and the truck they will need to go on.

10. The sharing that people must do to help each other survive in a harsh world.

Suggested Essay Topics

1. Trace the steps by which Tom Joad's character changes during his journey from Oklahoma to California.

2. Discuss the irony of the migrants who were driven from their hereditary home by drought being driven from even the temporary shelter they found by flooding rains.

Sample Analytical Paper Topics

The following paper topics are designed to test your understanding of the novel as a whole and to analyze important themes and literary devices. Following each question is a sample outline to get you started.

Topic #1

As the Joad clan begins to disintegrate under the pressure of migration, there is evidence to support that the family shifts from a patriarchal structure to a matriarchal one. Trace the progression of this change by analyzing and discussing key examples from the novel.

Outline

I. Thesis Statement: *Steinbeck shows Ma Joad as the strong force who realizes the true value and meaning of life.*

II. Patriarchal structure in early chapters

    A. Gathering to plan trip

    B. Posture and position of men

    C. Location of women

III. Focus of family life changes to truck

    A. Contents of truck

    B. Orders issued by Ma

    C. Eyes of characters predict change

IV. Ma asserts authority

    A. Incident of jack handle

    B. Savagery of California deputies

    C. Contradiction of Pa's feelings that "life's over and done with"

    D. Structure of life at Weedpatch

    E. Confrontation with camp manager

V. Ma takes actions

    A. Decides to move from camp

    B. Plans Tom's escape from the peach ranch

    C. Controls the family's money

    D. Finds work for the family

VI. Ma makes life and death decisions

    A. Leads family from boxcar

    B. Encourages Rose of Sharon to save a dying man

VII. Conclusion: Because of her personal strength and concerns

Ma Joad becomes the head of the family.

Topic #2

It has been implied by literary critics that Steinbeck uses Christianity and its traditions as a major base in his fiction, and that *The Grapes of Wrath* is both a parable and an allegory. Discuss this idea, giving examples from the novel that support this idea.

Outline

I.   Thesis Statement: *John Steinbeck's* The Grapes of Wrath *is a parable exploring Christian traditions.*

II. Characters—Family

    A.   Names with Biblical antecedents

    B.   Significance of family size

    C.   Family's connection with the earth

III. Christ-Casy relationship

    A.   Casy's whereabouts before entering book

    B.   Initials of name

    C.   Rejection of old religion

    D.   Knowledge of the "oversoul"

    E.   Acceptance of the sins of others

    F.   Circumstances of Casy's death

    G.   Tom as disciple

IV. Physical comparisons

    A.   Family driven from land by nature

    B.   People persecuted

    C.   Wander through life looking for a promised land

    D.   Survival of a great flood

V.   Symbolism

    A.   Title of novel

    B.   Casy's last words and death

    C.   Tom to carry on Casy's work

    D.   Rose of Sharon's gift of life

VI. Conclusion: Casy as the Christ figure gives up his life so that his message can live on.

Topic #3

The family is a universal symbol of the need for group effort and support to accomplish the greater good for the greater number of people. Trace the growth of the Joad family as they become members of the unity of all mankind.

Outline

I. Thesis Statement: *The Joads' journey west is also a journey from personal concerns to concern for all humanity.*

II. Family unit leaves Oklahoma

    A. Grampa, the individual, dies

    B. Granma dies

III. Family unit expands

    A. Casy joins the group

    B. Wilsons join with the Joads

    C. Families camp together at night

IV. Government camp

    A. Men create and enforce their own laws

    B. Women share ideas and resources

    C. Casy takes the blame for Tom

    D. People exchange information and help

    E. Ma feeds the hungry children

    F. Men share work with Tom

V. Cotton fields

    A. Joads share home with another family

    B.   Tom leaves to work for all humanity

    C.   All men work together to build dam

    D.   Rose of Sharon gives life to a dying man

VI. Conclusion: The economic decline of the Joad family is directly responsible for their acceptance of a larger humanitarian problem.

Topic #4

One prevalent theme of *The Grapes of Wrath* is the concept that strength comes from unity. Analyze situations in which Tom Joad, as a major protagonist, discovers and acts on this concept.

Outline

I.   Thesis Statement: *Steinbeck's development of Tom Joad's character reveals a major theme of the novel.*

II.   Tom's early background

    A.   Released from prison

    B.   No remorse for crime

    C.   Anxious for personal comfort

    D.   Refuses to hide on his own land

III. Treatment after release from prison

    A.   Individuality threatened

    B.   Independence threatened

    C.   Personal decency threatened

IV. Reactions and actions

    A.   Exposure to government camp

    B.   Kills again

    C. Recognizes importance of family unit

    D. Foregoes personal comforts

V. Considers Casy's philosophies

    A. Accepts all the world as a family

    B. Determines to carry out Casy's work in practical ways

VI. Conclusion: Tom realizes that all mankind is his family and without unity, this family has no power.

Topic #5

It has been suggested that *The Grapes of Wrath* is unique in that it encompasses the spectrum of all four literary conflicts. Discuss and give examples of the Joad family's encounters with

    1) man against man.

    2) man against society.

    3) man against nature.

    4) man against himself.

Outline

I. Thesis Statement: The Grapes Of Wrath *depicts ordinary people in their struggles to overcome a variety of conflicts.*

II. Man against man

    A. Tom kills in self-defense

    B. Men must buy inferior cars and parts

    C. Men must sell belongings for unfair prices

    D. Joads encounter policemen

    E. Development of land ownership in California

    F. Migrants turn against other migrants

G. Casy is killed for trying to organize the migrants

H. Tom kills again

III. Man against society

A. Tom is in prison for murder

B. Landowners are forced to evict tenants

C. Tom's parole modifies his actions

D. Coining of the word "Okie"

E. Families are forced to go to Tulare

F. Farmers' Association rules are imposed

G. Tom settles disputes with violence

IV. Man against nature

A. Oklahoma drought causes loss of home

B. Noah is injured at birth

C. Grampa dies

D. Granma dies

E. Rains cause flooding and loss of truck

F. Rose of Sharon becomes ill and loses baby

G. Flood drives Joads from temporary home

H. Rose of Sharon acts to save a dying man

V. Man against himself

A. Tom's reaction to the truck driver's curiosity

B. Casy's feelings about his preaching

C. Uncle John's self-punishment through guilt

D. Noah's feelings of being unloved

E. Ma's decision to feed the hungry children

F. Pa's depression and resignation

G. Rose of Sharon's worry that her baby will be born deformed

VI. Conclusion: *The Grapes of Wrath* explores all literary conflicts as the Joad family struggles to survive.

SECTION NINE

Bibliography

The following edition of the text was used for this study guide:

Steinbeck, John. *The Grapes of Wrath*. New York: Penguin
   Books USA Inc., 1976.

Introducing...

MAXnotes

REA's Literature Study Guide

MAXnotes™ offer a fresh look at masterpieces of literature, presented in a li
and interesting fashion. **MAXnotes**™ offer the essentials of what you should k
about the work, including outlines, explanations and discussions of the
character lists, analyses, and historical context. **MAXnotes**™ are designed to
you think independently about literary works by raising various issues and thou
provoking ideas and questions. Written by literary experts who currently teach
subject, **MAXnotes**™ enhance your understanding and enjoyment of the wor

---

Available **MAXnotes**™ include the following:

Animal Farm	**Huckleberry Finn**	**Of Mice and Men**
Beowulf	**I Know Why the**	**The Odyssey**
The Canterbury Tales	**Caged Bird Sings**	**Paradise Lost**
Death of a Salesman	**The Iliad**	**Plato's Republic**
Divine Comedy I-Inferno	**Julius Caesar**	**A Raisin in the Sun**
Gone with the Wind	**King Lear**	**Romeo and Juliet**
The Grapes of Wrath	**Les Misérables**	**The Scarlet Letter**
Great Expectations	**Macbeth**	**A Tale of Two Cities**
The Great Gatsby	**Moby Dick**	**To Kill a Mockingbird**
Hamlet	**1984**	

RESEARCH & EDUCATION ASSOCIATION
61 Ethel Road W. • Piscataway, New Jersey 08854
Phone: (908) 819-8880

Please send me more information about MAXnotes™.

Name _____

Address _____

City _____ State _____ Zip _____

The High School Tutors

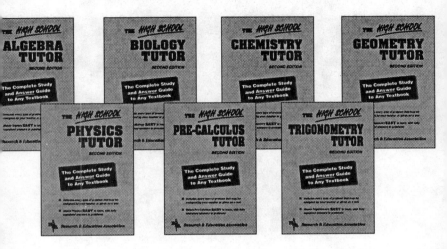

HIGH SCHOOL TUTORS series is based on the same principle as the more ‹om›prehensive **PROBLEM SOLVERS**, but is specifically designed to meet the needs of ‹high› school students. REA has recently revised all the books in this series to include expanded ‹n›ew sections, new material, and newly-designed covers. This makes the books even more ‹effe›ctive in helping students to cope with these difficult high school subjects.

If you would like more information about any of these books,
complete the coupon below and return it to us or go to your local bookstore.

RESEARCH & EDUCATION ASSOCIATION
‹6›1 Ethel Road W. • Piscataway, New Jersey 08854
Phone: (908) 819-8880

Please send me more information about your High School Tutor books.

‹N›ame _____

‹A›ddress _____

‹Ci›ty _____ State _____ Zip _____

REA's **VERBAL BUILDER**

for Admission & Standardized Tests

Specifically designed to prepare you for all tests requiring verbal ability, including

**GRE • GMAT • SAT
LSAT • ACT • MCAT • NTE
PPST • PSAT • CBEST**

Research & Education Association

Available at your local bookstore or order directly from us by sending in coupon below.

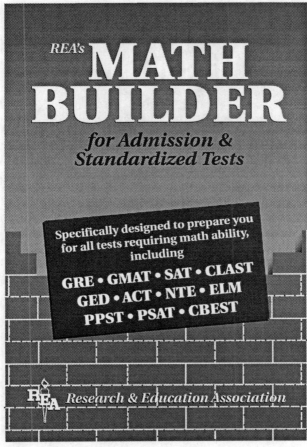